Crepes and Breads
SUNNY CARRANDI

Title: Crepes and Breads
2024 First Edition

Original text and recipes

Text and Photography: Sunny Carrandi

Cover and Layout Design: @Magaludesign

ISBN: 979-8-884-98391-5

Printed in United States
info@sunnycarrandi.com

It is strictly forbidden the total or partial reproduction of this work by any means or public loan

Thanks

I want to thank Luis Fernandez, my husband, for supporting me on every step I make, for your love, and most importantly, your patience. To Gaby Luque for pushing me to create this humble recipe book you are reading now, for her creativity and ideas to this project. To my children, Katty and Simon, you are the joy of my life.

As a software engineer who finds solace and joy in the art of cooking, particularly as a vegetarian fascinated by the intricate dance of nutrition and balanced diets, I humbly admit that I'm no culinary expert. Instead, I offer these recipes as humble reflections of my culinary journey, shared with those who share my passion for wholesome, gluten-free delights.

Currently transitioning into a new path as an aspiring Ayurveda practitioner, I welcome you to our cozy enclave of gluten-free indulgence, where the aroma of homemade crepes and breads beckons. This compilation of recipes is a product of love, stemming from my longing to provide delectable alternatives for fellow gluten-conscious individuals or those curious to venture into novel ingredients.

Throughout my culinary explorations, I've uncovered treasures within my kitchen— from the comforting textures of oats and millet flour to the surprising adaptability of lentils and chickpeas. Now, I'm thrilled to extend an invitation for you to join me on this gastronomic expedition!

Within the confines of these pages lie a treasury of meticulously crafted recipes, each intended to tantalize your taste buds and nurture your spirit. From crusty breads meant for communal sharing, lovingly baked to perfection, to savory crepes sizzling in a skillet, brimming with flavorful vegetables— there's an offering to suit every occasion and craving.

Regardless of whether you're a seasoned cook or just taking your first steps in the kitchen, I urge you to pull up a chair, don your apron, and embark on this flavorful voyage alongside me. Please let me know your thoughts. Don't hesitate to reach out. Together, let's delve into the enchanting realm of gluten-free crepes and breads, one modest recipe at a time. Prepare to fill your home with the irresistible scents of homemade goodness and partake in the joy of crafting meals that nourish both body and soul.

In addition to the recipes themselves, this cookbook serves as a compendium for unraveling the intricacies of gluten-free cuisine. While some recipes call for the warmth of the oven, resulting in delightful breads, others, like our delectable crepes, find their form in the embrace of a skillet. Throughout these pages, you'll discover invaluable tips and techniques ensuring your culinary endeavors yield perfection with each attempt. Whether you're kneading dough or perfecting that graceful flip, consider us your steadfast companions every step of the way.

Moreover, as we traverse these culinary pathways, let us not overlook the profound joy derived from sharing food with loved ones. Whether it's orchestrating a brunch affair with friends or simply surprising your family with a stack of freshly prepared crepes or a loaf of warm bread, the act of communal dining fosters bonds and memories destined to endure a lifetime.

Best Regards,

Sunny Carrandi

Contents

Gourmet Millet Flour Crepes 6
Almond Pancakes 10
Rice Crepes 14
Quinoa Crepes 18
Chickpeas Crepes 22
Rolled Oat Crepes 26
Spinach Crepes 30
Green Peas Bread 34
Pan de Bono 38
Lentil Crepes 42
Green Peas Crepes 46
Flaxseeds Pancakes 50
Broccoli Pancakes: 54
Cassava Croissants with Rolled Oats 58
Carrot Waffles 62
Lentil Bagels 66
Plantain Crepes 70
Morning Power Juice 74
Beets Juice 78
Delicious Summer Sanck 82
Creamy Shrimp Tacos 86
Peacock Fruit Salad 88
Palm Tree Fruit Salad 90
Green Pea Soup 92
Almond Banana Cake 94
Oats and Banana Cookies 96
Onion Soup 98
Glossary 100
Sources 123

Gourmet Millet Fluor Pancakes

Gourmet Millet Flour Pancakes

Millet flour emerges as an exceptional dietary choice for women, boasting an array of health benefits that cater to their specific needs. One notable advantage is its richness in iron, a vital nutrient crucial for maintaining healthy blood levels, particularly essential during menstruation. Alongside its iron content, millet flour is also abundant in dietary fiber, promoting digestive health while aiding in weight management. This fiber-rich nature not only supports overall well-being but also potentially lowers the risk of various digestive disorders, offering women a holistic approach to maintaining their health.

Furthermore, millet flour presents itself as a gluten-free alternative, making it a safe option for women with gluten sensitivities or celiac disease. This characteristic ensures that individuals with gluten-related concerns can still indulge in nutritious and delicious foods without compromising their dietary restrictions. In addition to being gluten-free, millet flour is packed with essential nutrients such as magnesium, phosphorus, and B vitamins, which are instrumental in supporting various bodily functions. These nutrients contribute to overall vitality and provide women with a wholesome dietary option to meet their nutritional requirements.

Research even suggests that millet may possess hormone-balancing properties, offering potential relief for women experiencing hormonal imbalances or navigating through menopause. This additional benefit underscores millet flour's significance as a versatile ingredient that not only nourishes the body but also addresses specific health concerns unique to women. Incorporating millet flour into one's diet, whether through homemade recipes like gourmet pancakes or other culinary creations, presents an enticing and nutritious way for women to harness its multitude of health advantages and enjoy a balanced and fulfilling lifestyle.

Incorporating millet flour into your diet can offer a range of health benefits and add diversity to your meals, making it a valuable addition to any pantry.

Ingredients

- 1 Ripe banana
- 1 Cup creamy oat milk
- 1 Cup high-quality millet flour
- 1/4 Cup rolled oats
- 1 Large egg
- Dash of vanilla extract
- Pinch of sea salt

Preparation

- Begin by mashing the ripe banana in a mixing bowl using a fork or spoon until smooth and creamy.
- Pour in the creamy oat milk and stir well to combine with the mashed banana, creating a luscious base for your pancakes.
- In a separate bowl, whisk together the high-quality millet flour, rolled oats, and a pinch of sea salt, ensuring even distribution of ingredients.
- Gradually blend the dry ingredients into the wet mixture, stirring gently until a smooth batter forms, ensuring no lumps remain.
- Crack a large egg into the batter, add a dash of vanilla extract, and continue mixing until fully incorporated, enhancing the flavor and texture of your pancakes.
- Heat a non-stick skillet or griddle over medium heat and lightly grease with cooking spray or butter. Pour the batter onto the skillet, using about 1/4 cup for each pancake, and cook until bubbles form on the surface, then flip and cook until golden brown and cooked through.
 Serve your fluffy pancakes warm, topped with your favorite syrup, a dollop of yogurt, and fresh berries for a delightful gourmet breakfast or brunch experience.

Prep time	Cook time	Total time	Serving
10 min	20 min	30 min	4-6 pancakes

Nutrition facts: 250-375 Calories, 10-15gr Protein, 40-60gr Carbs, 8-12gr Fat, 4-6gr Fiber

Almond Pancakes

Almond Pancakes

Almond flour pancakes offer a delectable and nourishing morning meal that caters to diverse tastes.

The advantages of incorporating almond flour into pancakes are abundant. Firstly, its innate gluten-free nature renders it ideal for individuals with gluten sensitivities or celiac disease, ensuring inclusivity without compromising on flavor or texture. Moreover, its reduced carbohydrate content compared to conventional wheat flour makes it a favored choice for adherents of low-carb or ketogenic diets, fostering dietary flexibility without sacrificing satisfaction.

Nutritionally, almond flour emerges as a powerhouse ingredient. Laden with essential nutrients including healthy fats, protein, fiber, and an array of vitamins and minerals such as vitamin E, magnesium, and calcium, its consumption not only bolsters overall health but also enhances the culinary experience. With a lower glycemic index than wheat flour, almond flour facilitates blood sugar regulation, proving beneficial for individuals managing diabetes or seeking to stabilize glucose levels. Additionally, its abundance of heart-healthy monounsaturated fats aids in cholesterol management, mitigating the risk of cardiovascular ailments while promoting satiety, thereby facilitating weight management efforts.

Incorporating almond flour into your pancake repertoire not only elevates taste but also embodies a conscious choice towards holistic well-being. Its versatility extends beyond the breakfast table, permeating into various culinary realms, from muffins to cookies and bread, enriching dishes with its nutty essence. Furthermore, its gentle digestibility, particularly for those with gluten sensitivities, underscores its culinary prowess, making almond flour pancakes a wholesome and gratifying indulgence for all palates.

Enjoy your delicious and nutritious almond flour pancakes! They're gluten-free, low-carb, and perfect for a delightful breakfast or brunch.

Ingredients

- 1 Cup almond flour
- 2 Tablespoons sweetener (e.g., granulated sugar, maple syrup, or honey)
- 1/2 Teaspoon baking powder
- 1/4 Teaspoon salt
- 2 Large eggs
- 1/4 Cup unsweetened almond milk (or any milk of your choice)
- 1 Teaspoon vanilla extract
- Butter or oil for greasing the pan

Optional toppings:
- Fresh berries
- Sliced bananas
- Maple syrup
- Greek yogurt
- Chopped nuts

> Nutrition facts: 320-480 Calories, 12-18gr Protein, 24-36gr Carbs, 24-36gr Fat, 4-6gr Fiber, 8-12gr Sugar

Preparation

- In a large mixing bowl, whisk together the almond flour, sweetener, baking powder, and salt until well combined.
- In a separate bowl, beat the eggs with a fork or whisk until they are well mixed.
- Add the beaten eggs, almond milk, and vanilla extract to the dry ingredients. Stir until the batter is smooth and no lumps remain.
- The batter should have a pourable consistency, similar to regular pancake batter. If it's too thick, you can add a little more almond milk to achieve the desired consistency.
- Preheat a non-stick skillet or griddle over medium heat. You can lightly grease the surface with butter or oil to prevent sticking.
- Once the skillet is hot, pour about 1/4 cup of the pancake batter onto the surface. You can make the pancakes larger or smaller, depending on your preference.
- Cook the pancakes for 2-3 minutes on the first side, or until you see bubbles forming on the surface.
- Carefully flip the pancake and cook for an additional 1-2 minutes on the other side, or until it's golden brown.
- Remove the cooked pancake from the skillet and keep it warm while you cook the rest of the batter. You can keep them warm in a preheated oven at 200°F (93°C) or cover them with a clean kitchen towel.
- Repeat the process with the remaining batter, adding more butter or oil to the skillet as needed.
- Serve the almond flour pancakes warm with your favorite toppings such as fresh berries, sliced bananas, maple syrup, Greek yogurt, or chopped nuts.

Prep time	Cook time	Total time	Serving
10 min	20 min	30 min	4-6 pancakes

Rice Crepes with a curry Twist

Rice Crepes with a curry Twist

Rice, a time-honored staple, boasts a rich history rooted in Asia, particularly in the ancient cultures of China and India. Its journey spans millennia, believed to have been cultivated some 10,000 years ago. Across the globe, rice manifests in various forms, from the familiar white grains to aromatic varieties like jasmine and basmati, each carrying its unique culinary charm. Beyond its role as a mere sustenance, rice stands as a versatile grain, offering not only a comforting taste but also a wealth of vital nutrients such as carbohydrates, vitamins, minerals, and fiber.

In the culinary realm, the amalgamation of rice and spices gives rise to the flavorful concoction known as curry rice, a beloved dish prevalent in Asian kitchens. The essence of this recipe lies in the harmonious blend of rice, spices, and sometimes vegetables or meats, concocting a dish that tantalizes the taste buds and evokes a sense of culinary adventure.

When considering the nutritional profile of Rice Crepes with a Curry Twist, one encounters a medley of benefits. Each serving, boasting approximately 225 kcal, serves as a reservoir of energy, ensuring vitality throughout daily endeavors. The carbohydrates, clocking in at around 29g per serving, stand tall as the primary fuel for the body, while the 8g of protein per portion aids in muscle repair and growth. With roughly 8g of fat, complemented by a modest 1g of fiber, these crepes offer a satisfying balance, further enriched by the subtle interplay of approximately 280mg of sodium, enhancing flavor without overpowering the palate.

In crafting these delectable crepes, the journey transcends mere ingredients, incorporating elements like eggs, water, and baking powder into the culinary tapestry. Eggs lend their protein prowess and moisture, water facilitates the attainment of the desired consistency, and baking powder bestows a light, airy texture upon the crepes. In the end, this recipe emerges not only as a symphony of flavors but also as a testament to the ingenuity of culinary innovation, offering a delightful and nutritious rendition of rice that promises to delight palates and nourish bodies alike.

Ingredients

- 1.5 Cups of cooked curry rice (leftovers work great!)
- 3 Eggs
- 3/4 Cup of water
- 1.5 Tbsp baking powder

Preparation

- In a blender, add the cooked curry rice, eggs, water, and baking powder.
- Blend the ingredients until you achieve a smooth and creamy consistency.
- Heat a non-stick skillet or crepe pan over medium heat and lightly grease it.
- Pour a small ladleful of the rice crepe batter onto the skillet and spread it evenly into a circular shape.
- Allow the crepe to cook for about 2-3 minutes, or until the edges start to slightly brown and the surface sets.
- Gently flip the crepe using a spatula and cook for an additional 1-2 minutes on the other side.
- Transfer the cooked crepe to a plate and repeat the process with the remaining batter.

Serving Suggestions:
Top your rice crepes with your favorite curry toppings, such as shredded chicken, vegetables, or even a dollop of yogurt. Get creative and have fun experimenting with different flavors!

Extra Tips:
Adjust the consistency of the batter by adding more water if needed. Feel free to season the batter with additional spices or herbs to complement the curry flavors.
These crepes can be enjoyed as a savory breakfast, a light lunch, or even as an appetizer for a dinner party.

Nutrition facts: 225 Calories, 8gr Protein, 29gr Carbs, 8gr Fat, 280mg Sodium

Prep time	Cook time	Total time	Serving
10 min	20 min	30 min	4-6 pancakes

Quinoa Crepes

Quinoa Crepes

Quinoa, a highly nutritious grain, offers numerous health benefits, making it an excellent choice for enhancing your meals and supporting your well-being. When used in recipes like Quinoa Crepes, it provides a rich source of protein, fiber, and essential nutrients. This versatile ingredient boasts a multitude of advantages, ranging from its high nutritional value to its gluten-free nature.

Quinoa is packed with essential nutrients such as protein, fiber, vitamins, and minerals, including magnesium, iron, and zinc. It offers a comprehensive array of nutrients necessary for overall health and well-being, making it a valuable addition to any diet. Additionally, being naturally gluten-free, quinoa provides a safe alternative to traditional grains like wheat, barley, and rye, Catering to individuals with gluten intolerance or celiac disease.

Moreover, quinoa stands out as a complete protein source, containing all nine essential amino acids required by the body. This quality makes it particularly beneficial for vegetarians and vegans seeking alternative protein sources. Furthermore, its inclusion in your diet can contribute to improved heart health, digestive health, and weight management, thanks to its heart-healthy fats, antioxidants, and high fiber content.

Incorporating quinoa into your meals not only adds delightful flavor and texture but also supports your overall health and well-being, making it a versatile and nutritious choice for any culinary adventure.

Note: Quinoa Crepes are best enjoyed fresh but can be stored in an airtight container in the refrigerator for up to 2 days. Reheat gently in a skillet or microwave before serving, if desired.

Ingredients

- 1 Cup soaked quinoa
- 1 Egg
- Pinch of pink salt
- 1 Cup water or as needed
- 1 Tbsp baking powder

Preparation

- Soak the quinoa the night before preparation or for 6 hours prior to preparation
- Prepare the Quinoa Batter:
    - Rinse the soaked quinoa thoroughly under cold water to remove any residual bitterness.
    - In a blender or food processor, combine the soaked quinoa, egg, pinch of pink salt, and a small amount of water.
    - Blend until smooth, adding more water as needed to achieve a pourable consistency similar to pancake batter.
- Cook the Crepes:
    - Heat a non-stick skillet or crepe pan over medium heat.
    - Lightly grease the pan with cooking spray or a small amount of oil.
    - Pour a ladleful of the quinoa batter into the center of the pan, swirling it around to evenly coat the bottom in a thin layer.
    - Cook the crepe for 2-3 minutes, or until the edges start to lift and the bottom is golden brown.
    - Carefully flip the crepe using a spatula and cook for an additional 1-2 minutes on the other side.
    - Repeat with the remaining batter, greasing the pan as needed between crepes.
- Serve and Enjoy:
    - Once cooked, transfer the crepes to a plate and serve warm.
    - These Quinoa Crepes can be enjoyed plain or filled with your favorite sweet or savory toppings such as fresh fruit, yogurt, honey, Nutella, vegetables, cheese, or herbs.

Enjoy your delicious and nutritious Quinoa Crepes!

Nutrition facts: 440 Calories, 20gr Protein, 23gr Carbs, 280gr Fat, 622mg Sodium

Prep time	Cook time	Total time	Serving
10 min	20 min	30 min	4-6 pancakes

Chickpeas Crepes

Chickpeas Crepes

Chickpeas, the main ingredient in these Protein Chickpea Crepes, offer numerous health benefits. These legumes are packed with protein, making them an excellent choice for vegetarians and vegans looking to meet their protein needs. Additionally, chickpeas are rich in fiber, which aids in digestion and helps to keep you feeling full and satisfied. This recipe provides a substantial amount of protein (~10g per serving) and fiber (5g per serving), which can contribute to satiety and weight management.

Furthermore, chickpeas are a good source of carbohydrates, providing sustained energy levels without causing spikes in blood sugar. They also contain essential vitamins and minerals, including iron, magnesium, and folate. Incorporating chickpeas into your diet can support heart health, regulate blood sugar levels, and improve overall digestive health. By using chickpeas as the base for these crepes, you can enjoy a nutritious and satisfying meal that is both delicious and beneficial for your health.

Moreover, chickpeas are versatile and can be incorporated into various dishes, ranging from salads and soups to snacks and desserts. This adaptability makes them a convenient and accessible ingredient for anyone looking to boost their nutritional intake. Whether roasted for a crunchy snack or blended into a creamy hummus, chickpeas offer endless possibilities for culinary exploration.

In addition to their nutritional value, chickpeas are also environmentally friendly. As legumes, they have a lower environmental footprint compared to animal-based protein sources. Chickpea cultivation typically requires less water and produces fewer greenhouse gas emissions, making them a sustainable option for both human health and the planet. By choosing recipes like these Protein Chickpea Crepes, individuals can play a part in promoting sustainable food practices while enjoying a delicious and nourishing meal.

Enjoy your delicious and protein-packed chickpea crepes! These nutritious and versatile crepes are perfect for a hearty breakfast, a quick snack, or a light lunch. Experiment with different fillings to create your favorite combinations!

Ingredients

- 2 Cups of soaked chickpeas
- 1 Cup of water
- Salt, to taste
- 1 Tablespoon baking powder

Preparation

- Soak chickpeas overnight or for 6 hours. Drain and rinse well.
- Blend chickpeas until smooth. Add water gradually until batter is pourable.
- Transfer batter to a bowl. Mix in salt (start with 1/2 tsp) and baking powder.
- Crack egg into batter and whisk well.
- Heat a non-stick pan over medium heat. Pour 1/4 cup batter, swirl to spread.
- Cook for 2-3 mins until edges golden, then flip and cook 1-2 mins more.
- Repeat with remaining batter.
- Serve warm with desired toppings.

Prep time	Cook time	Total time	Serving
15 min	9 min	24 min	6-8 ud

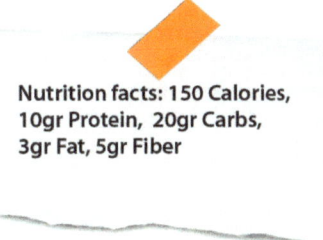

Nutrition facts: 150 Calories, 10gr Protein, 20gr Carbs, 3gr Fat, 5gr Fiber

Rolled Oat Crepes

Rolled Oat Crepes

Oats are a versatile and nutritious ingredient that offer numerous health benefits. In this wholesome oatmeal tortillas recipe, oats are the star ingredient, providing a variety of advantages. Firstly, oats are a great source of dietary fiber, which helps promote digestive health and keeps you feeling fuller for longer periods, making these tortillas a satisfying meal option. Additionally, oats contain essential vitamins and minerals such as iron, magnesium, and B vitamins, contributing to overall well-being and energy levels. The inclusion of oat flour in these tortillas adds a unique texture and flavor while also making them suitable for individuals with gluten sensitivities, as oats are naturally gluten-free. Furthermore, oats are known to support heart health by helping to lower cholesterol levels and reduce the risk of cardiovascular diseases. With just a few simple ingredients like oat flour, egg, water, salt, and baking powder, these oatmeal tortillas offer a convenient and delicious way to incorporate the benefits of oats into your diet. Whether enjoyed as a wrap for savory or sweet fillings, these tortillas are a wholesome and nutritious choice for any meal.

Moreover, the complex carbohydrates present in oats provide a sustained release of energy, making them an excellent choice for maintaining steady blood sugar levels throughout the day. This makes these oatmeal tortillas not only a satisfying option but also a smart choice for those looking to manage their weight or control their sugar intake. By incorporating oats into your diet through dishes like these tortillas, you can support your overall health goals while enjoying a delicious and filling meal.

Beyond their nutritional benefits, oats are also celebrated for their versatility in the kitchen. From breakfast bowls to baked goods, oats can be incorporated into a wide range of recipes to boost their nutritional profile and add a hearty texture. These oatmeal tortillas showcase just how adaptable oats can be, providing a wholesome alternative to traditional flour-based tortillas without sacrificing taste or texture. Whether you're following a gluten-free diet or simply looking to add more fiber-rich foods to your meals, these oatmeal tortillas offer a delicious solution that's sure to become a staple in your kitchen repertoire.

Prep time	Cook time	Total time	Serving
15 min	9 min	24 min	4-6 crepes

These oatmeal tortillas are a perfect way to add wholesome goodness to your meals while keeping things tasty. Give them a try and let us know how you enjoy them! #OatmealTortillas #HealthyEating #DeliciouslyWholesome

Ingredients

- 1 3/4 Cups oat flour (simply blend rolled oats until they become a fine powder)
- 1 Egg
- 1 1/2 Cups water
- Pinch of salt
- 1 Tsp baking powder

Craving a nutritious twist on your favorite wraps? Look no further! These homemade oatmeal tortillas are packed with goodness and

Preparation

- In a large mixing bowl, combine 1 3/4 cups oat flour, 1 egg, 1 1/2 cups water, a pinch of salt, and 1 tsp baking powder. Stir until all the ingredients are well incorporated.
- Let the mixture rest for 5 minutes, allowing the oat flour to absorb the liquid and create a dough-like consistency.
- Meanwhile, preheat a non-stick skillet or griddle over medium heat. Make sure it's evenly heated to prevent sticking.
- Once hot, lightly grease the skillet with cooking spray or a touch of oil. Pour approximately 1/4 cup of the oatmeal mixture onto the skillet, forming a circular shape. Spread it out using the back of a ladle or spoon.
- Cook the tortilla for 2-3 minutes on one side until small bubbles appear on the surface. Flip it over using a spatula and cook for another 1-2 minutes until golden brown on both sides.
- Transfer the cooked tortilla to a plate and repeat the process with the remaining oatmeal mixture. Adjust the heat as needed to avoid burning.
- Fill these versatile tortillas with your favorite ingredients like grilled veggies, chicken, or beans to create scrumptious wraps and tacos. You can even enjoy them on their own as a light breakfast or snack.

Note: Nutrition facts are approximate and may vary based on the specific brands and quantities of ingredients used.

Pro tip: Customize your tortillas by adding herbs or spices like garlic powder, cumin, or chili flakes for an extra flavor kick!

Nutrition facts: 100 Calories, 4gr Protein, 14gr Carbs, 3gr Fat, 160mg Sodium

Spinach Crepes

Spinach Crepes

The recipe presented is for Gourmet Spinach Crepes with Melted Munster Cheese, a delectable dish that promises to delight the senses. It combines the freshness of spinach, the richness of free-range eggs, and the smoothness of Munster cheese to create a harmonious culinary experience. The ingredients required include fresh spinach, free-range eggs, all-purpose flour, whole milk, baking powder, salt, and slices of Munster cheese. This dish offers a unique fusion of flavors and textures, showcasing the artistry of gourmet cooking.

Welcome to a world of culinary enchantment! In this recipe book, I present to you a true masterpiece of flavors and textures—my Gourmet Spinach Crepes with Melted Munster Cheese. These delightful crepes are a testament to the art of gourmet cooking, where the fusion of vibrant spinach, free-range eggs, and the silky Munster cheese create a symphony that will captivate your taste buds and leave you utterly enchanted. Get ready to embark on a gastronomic adventure like no other!

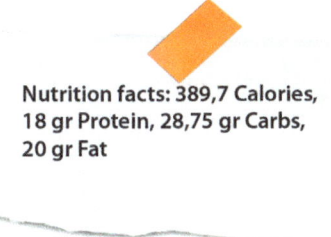

Nutrition facts: 389,7 Calories, 18 gr Protein, 28,75 gr Carbs, 20 gr Fat

Prep time	Cook time	Total time	Serving
15 min	9 min	24 min	4-6 crepes

Savor the enchanting flavors with a light and crisp white wine, and let the magic of these crepes transport you to a world of epicurean bliss. Share this extraordinary experience with your loved ones, and they'll be yearning for more. Embrace the green hues, relish the delicate textures, and immerse yourself in the captivating symphony of flavors offered by these exquisite crepes. Happy cooking!

Ingredients

- 2 Cups fresh spinach, washed and finely chopped
- 4 Large free-range eggs
- 1 Cup all-purpose flour
- 1 ½ Cups whole milk
- ¼ Teaspoon baking powder
- Pinch of salt
- 6 Slices Munster cheese

Preparation

- In a blender or food processor, combine the chopped spinach and free-range eggs. Blend until you have a smooth, vibrant green mixture.
- In a mixing bowl, whisk together the flour, milk, and baking powder until you have a lump-free, thin batter. Incorporate the spinach and egg mixture into the batter, stirring gently until fully combined.
- Heat a non-stick skillet over medium heat. Pour approximately 1/4 cup of the crepe batter onto the skillet and swirl it around to create a thin, even layer. Cook the crepe for about 2 minutes on each side or until lightly golden.
- As each crepe finishes cooking, place a slice of Munster cheese in the center and fold the crepe into a quarter-circle shape, allowing the cheese to melt within.
- Repeat the process until you have six delicious Spinach Crepes with Melted Munster Cheese.

Congratulations! You've now mastered the art of creating Gourmet Spinach Crepes with Melted Munster Cheese. With each bite, you'll experience the delightful harmony of fresh spinach, velvety crepes, and creamy Munster cheese. These culinary marvels are perfect for indulging in a luxurious brunch or impressing guests with a sophisticated appetizer.

Green Peas Bread

Green Peas Bread

Green Peas Bread introduces a plethora of benefits through its innovative combination of soaked green peas, vegan yogurt, eggs, salt, and baking powder.

This delightful creation not only tantalizes the taste buds with a symphony of flavors but also offers numerous health benefits. Green peas, known for their vibrant green hues, are rich in essential nutrients such as fiber, vitamins, and minerals.

They contribute to digestive health, heart health, and weight management. Additionally, the inclusion of vegan yogurt adds a creamy texture while catering to dietary preferences. Eggs provide a source of high-quality protein and essential amino acids.

A pinch of salt enhances flavor while baking powder ensures a light and fluffy texture. Overall, Green Peas Bread offers a delectable way to enjoy the nutritional goodness of green peas while savoring a unique culinary experience.

Nutrition facts: 280 Calories, 13gr Protein, 25gr Carbs, 15gr Fat, 4gr Fiber

Prep time	Cook time	Total time	Serving
15 min	9 min	24 min	4-6 people

Get ready to savor the taste of fresh green peas in every bite of our delicious bread! Snap a picture, take a bite, at let is know what you think. Don't forget to tag us @sunnysalads and use #GreenPeasBread for a chance to be featured!

Get ready to embark on a gourmet adventure like no other!
Enjoy the delightful Green Peas Bread and share this incredible recipe with your loved ones.

Ingredients

- Soaked green peas (overnight for tenderness)
- Vegan yogurt
- Eggs
- Pinch of salt
- Baking powder

Prepare to be amazed by this delightful creation that combines the vibrant hues of green peas with a symphony of flavors.

With just a handful of premium ingredients, we've created a masterpiece that will tantalize your taste buds. Watch as the green peas, with their tender texture, blend effortlessly with the creamy vegan yogurt and eggs, creating a velvety mixture that's as beautiful as it is delicious.

Preparation

- Soak the green peas overnight to achieve the perfect tenderness.
- In a blender, combine the soaked green peas, vegan yogurt, eggs, pinch of salt, and baking powder. Blend until you have a smooth and luscious green mixture.
- Pour the prepared mixture into a loaf pan, ensuring it is evenly spread.
- Preheat your oven to 350°F (175°C) and carefully place the loaf pan inside. Bake the Green Peas Bread for about 50 minutes, or until it rises gracefully and acquires a golden crust that adds a delightful crunch to every bite.
- Each slice of this Green Peas Bread reveals a symphony of flavors, where the sweetness of green peas harmonizes with the tangy notes of vegan yogurt, while the eggs add a touch of richness, and the pinch of salt enhances the overall taste.
- Elevate your culinary journey with this gourmet creation and indulge in the enchanting flavors of Green Peas Bread. Trust us, you won't be able to resist its captivating taste!
- Snap a picture, take a bite, and let us know what you think! Don't forget to tag us and use #GreenPeasBread for a chance to be featured!
- Get ready to embark on a gourmet adventure like no other! Enjoy the delightful Green Peas Bread and share this incredible recipe with your loved ones. Happy baking!

Pan de Bono

Pan de Bono

Cassava, a versatile root vegetable, offers numerous benefits in culinary applications. By incorporating 1-1/2 cups of cassava flour into recipes, such as the one provided, you can enjoy its various advantages. Cassava flour is naturally gluten-free, making it suitable for individuals with gluten sensitivities or celiac disease. Additionally, it contains essential nutrients like fiber, vitamins, and minerals, contributing to a balanced diet.

In this recipe, cassava flour is combined with other ingredients like corn flour, baking powder, salt, sugar, egg, melted butter, and milk to create a delicious dough. Cassava flour enhances the texture of the dough, providing a light and airy consistency to the final product. Moreover, cassava flour adds a subtle sweetness and nutty flavor to the dough, enhancing the overall taste of the dish.

Furthermore, the addition of cassava flour helps bind the ingredients together, ensuring proper structure and consistency. This property is particularly beneficial when making dough for dishes like cheese balls, as it helps maintain their shape during baking.

Moreover, cassava flour can be paired with various types of cheese, such as mozzarella, salted white cheese, and your preferred cheese for covering each ball. The combination of cassava flour and cheese results in a flavorful and satisfying snack or appetizer.

Overall, incorporating cassava flour into recipes provides a range of benefits, including gluten-free properties, nutritional value, improved texture, and enhanced flavor. With its versatility and numerous advantages, cassava flour is a valuable ingredient in the culinary world.

Prep time	Cook time	Total time	Serving
30 min	30 min	1 hour	6 people

Ingredients

1-1/2 Cup of cassava flour
1/2 Cup of pan flour (corn flour)
1 Teaspoon of baking powder
1/2 Teaspoon of salt
2 Tablespoons of sugar
1 Egg
3 Tablespoons of melted butter
3/4 Cup of milk

1 Cup of mozzarella cheese
1 Cup of salted white cheese
1/4 Cup of your preferred cheese to cover each ball
Wax paper
Cookie oven tray

Amount of cheese bread: 12 small units (64 g each)
Baking temperature: 400°F (204°C)
Baking time: 25 minutes.

Preparation

- Preheat the oven to 400°F.
- Place a wax sheet on the cookie oven tray.
- In a large bowl, combine the cassava flour, pan flour, baking powder, salt, sugar, egg, salted white cheese, mozzarella cheese, and melted butter.
- Begin kneading the dough and gradually incorporate the milk.
- Continue kneading the dough until it reaches a manageable consistency and you can form small balls.
- Roll each ball in the chosen shredded cheese.
- Arrange the balls on the oven tray.
- Bake in the oven for 25 minutes.

Nutrition facts: 166,3 Calories, 4,42gr Protein, 23,53gr Carbs, 5,92gr Fat, 109,2mg Sodium, 1,68 gr Sugar

Enjoy your delicious treats!

Lentil Crepes

Lentil Crepes

Lentils offer a range of health benefits, and incorporating them into your breakfast routine with protein-packed lentil crepes can be a smart choice. These crepes are not only delicious but also nutritious, with just four simple ingredients. With each serving containing only 126 calories per crepe, they provide a guilt-free indulgence. Lentils are rich in protein, making them a great addition to any meal, especially breakfast, as they can help keep you feeling full and satisfied throughout the morning. Additionally, lentils are packed with fiber, vitamins, and minerals, contributing to overall health and well-being. Try these lentil crepes as a healthy breakfast option and experience the benefits for yourself.

Note: You can store any leftover crepes in an airtight container in the refrigerator for up to three days. Simply reheat them in a lightly greased pan before serving.

Calorie-Conscious Tip:
To further reduce calories, you can skip the egg and use a flax egg (1 tablespoon ground flaxseed mixed with 3 tablespoons water) as a vegan alternative.

Nutrition facts : 90 Calories, 4gr Protein, 13gr Carbs, 3gr Fat, 210mg Sodium, 4gr Sugar, 40 mg Cholesterol

Prep time	Cook time	Total time	Serving
15 min	9 min	24 min	6 crepes

Conclusion:
These lentil crepes are not only delicious but also a fantastic source of plant-based protein and essential nutrients. Make them a regular part of your breakfast routine.

Ingredients

- 1 cup lentils
- 1 cup water
- 1 egg
- Pinch of salt

Start your day right with these protein-packed lentil crepes! Made with just four simple ingredients, this nutritious recipe is a perfect addition to your breakfast routine. Each serving contains only 126 calories per crepe, making it a guilt-free indulgence. Try it out and let us know what you think!

Preparation

- Rinse the lentils thoroughly under cold water, then place them in a bowl and cover with water. Allow them to soak for about 2 hours, or overnight if preferred.
- Drain the lentils and transfer them to a blender or food processor. Add the water, egg, and pinch of salt. Blend until you have a smooth batter.
- Preheat a non-stick skillet or crepe pan over medium heat. Lightly grease it with cooking spray or a small amount of oil.
- Pour ¼ cup of the lentil batter onto the skillet, tilting it in a circular motion to evenly spread the batter into a thin crepe.
- Cook for about 2-3 minutes, or until the edges start to lift and the bottom is golden brown.
- Flip the crepe using a spatula and cook for another 1-2 minutes on the other side until it turns golden brown.
- Transfer the cooked crepe to a plate and repeat the process with the remaining batter until all crepes are cooked.
- Serve the lentil crepes warm with your favorite toppings, such as fresh fruits, Greek yogurt, honey, or nut butter.
- Enjoy your protein-packed lentil crepes!

Green Peas Crepes

Green Peas Crepes

Green peas, known botanically as Pisum sativum, are a popular legume that has been cultivated for thousands of years. Originating in the Mediterranean region, green peas have been a staple in diets worldwide due to their versatility, nutritional value, and delicious flavor.

This recipe for Green Peas Crepes offers a creative and healthy twist on traditional crepes by incorporating green peas as a primary ingredient. Green peas are rich in protein, making them an excellent plant-based source of this essential nutrient. Additionally, they are packed with vitamins, minerals, and dietary fiber, contributing to overall health and well-being.

The crepes are made by blending green peas with oat flakes, coconut milk, eggs, baking powder, and salt until smooth. This combination creates a batter that is then cooked like traditional crepes on a hot pan with a bit of coconut oil. Once cooked to golden brown perfection, the crepes can be topped with shredded Mexican cheese or any preferred toppings before being folded and served.

In terms of nutrition, each serving of these Green Peas Crepes provides approximately 280 calories, 13 grams of protein, 25 grams of carbohydrates, 15 grams of fat, and 4 grams of fiber. These crepes are not only delicious but also offer a balanced nutritional profile that can be enjoyed for any meal of the day.

Prep time	Cook time	Total time	Serving
15 min	9 min	24 min	4-6 pancakes

Ingredients

- 1 cup of green peas
- 1/2 cup of oat flakes
- 1 cup of coconut milk
- 2 eggs
- 2 tbsp of baking powder
- Salt to taste

Indulge in a healthy twist with these Green Peas Crepes! Packed with protein and flavor, they're perfect for any meal of the day. Here's how to whip them up:

Preparation

- Combine all ingredients in your blender until smooth. Heat a pan and add a dollop of coconut oil.
- Pour a ladleful of batter onto the pan and swirl to spread evenly.
- Cook until bubbles form on the surface, then flip and cook until golden brown.
- Top with shredded Mexican cheese or your favorite toppings, then fold and serve.

Prep time	Cook time	Total time	Serving
15 min	9 min	24 min	4-6 pancakes

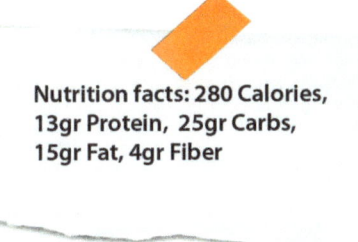

Nutrition facts: 280 Calories, 13gr Protein, 25gr Carbs, 15gr Fat, 4gr Fiber

Flaxseeds Pancakes

Flaxseed, rich in omega-3 fatty acids, fiber, and lignans, offers a multitude of health benefits. Firstly, its abundance of alpha-linolenic acid (ALA), a vital omega-3 fatty acid, supports cardiovascular health, cognitive function, and diminishes bodily inflammation. Additionally, its high fiber content, comprising both soluble and insoluble fibers, aids in stabilizing blood sugar levels, reducing cholesterol, and promoting optimal digestion by enhancing stool bulk and preventing constipation. Moreover, the presence of lignans imbues flaxseed with potent antioxidant properties, combating free radicals to mitigate the risk of chronic ailments like heart disease and certain cancers.

Beyond its nutritional prowess, flaxseed presents practical advantages in dietary alternatives. For instance, flaxseed meal serves as a low-carbohydrate substitute for traditional flour in recipes, especially beneficial for adherents of low-carb or ketogenic diets seeking healthier options. Moreover, its inherent gluten-free nature renders it suitable for individuals with gluten sensitivities or celiac disease, broadening its accessibility in diverse dietary preferences. By incorporating flaxseed, such as utilizing flaxseed meal in pancake recipes, individuals can proactively foster better heart health, bolster digestion, and enhance overall well-being.

In conclusion, embracing flaxseed as a dietary staple yields multifaceted benefits, encompassing cardiovascular support, digestive wellness, and disease prevention. Whether enjoyed in the form of flaxseed meal pancakes or integrated creatively into various culinary endeavors, its nutritional richness and functional versatility make it a valuable addition to any balanced diet. By harnessing the power of flaxseed, individuals can embark on a journey towards improved health and vitality, unlocking its transformative potential in fostering holistic well-being.

Nutrition facts: 231 Calories, 11,83gr Protein, 13,8gr Carbs, 6,75gr Fat

Voila! You've created a stack of delectable flaxseed pancakes that are not only visually appealing but also packed with wholesome goodness. Serve them hot with your favorite toppings like fresh berries, maple syrup, or a dollop of Greek yogurt. Whether it's breakfast, brunch, or a midnight snack, these pancakes are sure to impress and satisfy. Enjoy every fluffy bite and revel in the satisfaction of indulging in a nutritious treat.

Ingredients

- 1 Cup flaxseed meal
- 4 Eggs, beaten
- 1/3 Cup unsweetened almond milk (or other milk)
- 1 Tbsp lemon juice
- 1 Tsp baking soda
- 1 Tsp vanilla extract
- 1 Tsp cinnamon
- 1/8 Tsp salt

Preparation

- Now that you have everything ready, let's dive into the cooking process:
- Begin by heating a skillet over medium heat. This step is crucial for achieving that perfect golden-brown exterior while maintaining a fluffy interior.
- Once the skillet is adequately heated, generously spray it with cooking spray or add a small amount of cooking oil. This ensures your pancakes won't stick and facilitates an even cooking surface.
- In a mixing bowl, combine the flaxseed meal, beaten eggs, almond milk, lemon juice, baking soda, vanilla extract, cinnamon, and salt.
- Stir the ingredients together until they form a smooth and homogeneous batter.
- Now, the fun part begins. Pour approximately 1/4 cup of the batter onto the skillet for each pancake. Using the back of a spoon, gently spread the batter out to form a uniform circle. This step ensures even cooking and uniform thickness.
- Allow the pancakes to cook undisturbed for 2-3 minutes on one side. Keep a keen eye on the edges; once they start to firm up and bubbles form on the surface, it's time to flip.
- Carefully flip each pancake using a spatula and cook for an additional 2-3 minutes on the opposite side. This ensures that both sides are perfectly golden brown and cooked through.
- Once cooked to perfection, transfer the pancakes to a plate and repeat the process with the remaining batter.

Prep time	Cook time	Total time	Serving
5-10 min	20 min	30 min	4-6 pancakes

Broccoli Pancakes

Broccoli Pancakes

Broccoli pancakes present a delightful fusion flavors and nutrients, seamlessly blending the goodness of broccoli with the comfort of pancakes. Packed with vitamins C, K, and A, as well as folate, fiber, and antioxidants, these pancakes offer a substantial nutritional boost to any meal. The incorporation of broccoli not only enhances the taste but also elevates the health
profile of the dish, making it a smart choice for those seeking to infuse their diet with more wholesome ingredients.

The high fiber content of oats in the recipe promotes digestive health, aids in managing blood sugar levels, and fosters a feeling of fullness, contributing to overall well-being. Additionally, being naturally gluten-free, these pancakes cater to individuals with gluten sensitivities, expanding the accessibility of nutritious options in dietary choices. This gluten-free attribute, coupled with their relatively low-calorie nature, makes broccoli pancakes an appealing choice for those mindful of their calorie intake without compromising on taste or satisfaction.

Beyond their nutritional benefits, broccoli pancakes offer a canvas for culinary creativity, accommodating various toppings to suit diverse preferences. From savory options like salsa and avocado to sweet indulgences like yogurt and maple syrup, the versatility of these pancakes knows no bounds. With simple ingredients and easy preparation techniques, they offer a fuss-free solution for home cooks of all levels, while their vegetarian and plant-based nature ensures they're a wholesome addition to any diet. In essence, broccoli pancakes embody the perfect blend of flavor, nutrition, and convenience, making them a delightful choice for any meal occasion.

Prep time	Cook time	Total time	Serving
5-10 min	20 min	30 min	4-6 pancakes

Please note that these values are approximate and may vary based on factors such as the exact ingredients used and any additional toppings or modifications made to the recipe.
Additionally, it's important to adjust these values based on the serving size you consume.
Enjoy your nutritious and delicious broccoli pancakes!

Ingredients

- 2 Cups raw broccoli, chopped
- 2 Cups water
- 2 Cups old-fashioned oat flakes
- Himalayan salt, to taste
- 1 Tablespoon baking powder

Preparation

- Prepare the Broccoli: Rinse the raw broccoli under cold water. Cut it into smaller florets to ensure even blending.
- Blend Broccoli: In a blender, combine the chopped broccoli and water. Blend until smooth.
- Mix Dry Ingredients: In a large mixing bowl, combine the oat flakes, Himalayan salt, and baking powder.
- Combine Wet and Dry Ingredients: Pour the blended broccoli mixture into the bowl with the dry ingredients. Mix well until a smooth batter forms.
- Let the Batter Rest: Allow the batter to rest for about 10-15 min. This allows the oats to absorb some of the moisture and thicken the batter slightly.
- Cook the Pancakes: Heat a non-stick skillet or griddle over medium heat. Lightly grease the surface with oil or cooking spray.
- Cooking: Pour a ladleful of batter onto the skillet, spreading it out gently with the back of the ladle to form a thin pancake. Cook for 2-3 minutes, or until bubbles form on the surface and the edges start to look set.
- Flip and Cook: Carefully flip the pancake using a spatula and cook for an additional 1-2 min on the other side, or until lightly golden brown and cooked through.
- Repeat: Continue cooking the remaining batter in batches, adding more oil to the skillet as needed, until all the batter is used.
- Serve: Serve the broccoli pancakes warm, topped with your favorite toppings such as yogurt, salsa, avocado slices, or a drizzle of maple syrup.

Nutrition facts: 860 Calories, 32gr Protein, 140gr Carbs, 17gr Fat, 24gr Fiber

Cassava Croissants with Rolled Oats

Cassava Croissants with Rolled Oats

Welcome to the world of culinary creativity, where classic flavors meet innovative twists. In this recipe, we'll be crafting a delightful fusion of textures and tastes with our yuca Croissants with Oat Flakes. These golden, flaky pastries marry the comforting familiarity of yuca with the wholesome crunch of oat flakes, resulting in a treat that's as visually stunning as it is delicious.

By blending the mild sweetness of yuca with the nutty essence of oat flakes, these croissants offer a unique flavor profile that's sure to tantalize the taste buds. Utilizing frozen yuca and oat flakes, this recipe champions wholesome, natural ingredients, making it a nourishing option for any occasion. The contrast between the soft, pillow interior of the yuca and the crisp, flaky layers of the croissant creates a textural experience that's nothing short of sensational. Plus, with just a handful of ingredients and straightforward steps, these croissants are surprisingly easy to make, allowing you to impress friends and family with minimal effort. Whether enjoyed as a savory breakfast option or served alongside a cup of tea for a delightful afternoon snack, these yuca croissants with oat flakes are endlessly versatile, adapting effortlessly to any culinary setting.

Indulge your senses and embark on a culinary adventure as we dive into the recipe for these delectable Yuca Croissants with Oat Flakes.

Happy baking!

Nutrition facts: 71 Calories, 2,195gr Protein, 13,89gr Carbs, 119,44gr Fat, 1,3gr Fiber

Prep time	Cook time	Total time	Serving
20 min	20 min	40 min	8-10 croissant

These yuca croissants have a unique flavor and texture, thanks to the combination of yuca
flour and oat flakes. Enjoy this gluten-free twist on a classic pastry!

Happy baking!

Ingredients

- 1 Cup of frozen yuca
- 1 Cup oat flakes (rolled oats)
- 1/2 Teaspoon salt
- 1/2 Cup cold butter, cubed
- 1/2 Cup cold water
- 1 Egg (for egg wash)

Preparation

Prepare the Dough:
- In a mixing bowl, combine the yuca flour, oat flakes, and salt.
- Add the cold, cubed butter to the dry ingredients. Use your fingers or a pastry cutter to work the butter into the flour mixture until it resembles coarse crumbs.
- Gradually add the cold water, a little at a time, and mix until the dough comes together. It should be slightly sticky but manageable. If needed, adjust the water or flour to achieve the right consistency.

Roll and Fold:
- Dust your work surface with additional yuca flour.
- Roll out the dough into a rectangle, about 1/4 inch thick.
- Fold the dough into thirds, like a letter. This creates layers in the croissant.
- Rotate the dough 90 degrees and roll it out again. Fold into thirds once more.
- Repeat this rolling and folding process 3-4 times to create flaky layers.

Shape the Croissants:
- Preheat your oven to 375°F (190°C).
- Roll out the dough one final time into a large rectangle.
- Cut the dough into triangles (like traditional croissants).
- Starting from the wide end, roll each triangle toward the pointed end to form a croissant shape.
- Place the croissants on a baking sheet lined with parchment paper.

Egg Wash and Bake:
- Beat the egg and brush it over the tops of the croissants. This gives them a beautiful golden color when baked.
- Bake in the preheated oven for 20-25 minutes or until the croissants are puffed up and golden brown. Enjoy!
- Let the yuca croissants cool slightly before serving.
- Serve them warm with your favorite spreads, such as butter, jam, or honey.

Carrot Waffles

Carrot Waffles

Welcome to a delightful twist on a breakfast classic - Carrot Waffles! These golden-brown beauties are not only a treat for your taste buds but also pack a punch of nutrition to kickstart your day. Packed with wholesome ingredients and bursting with flavor, these waffles are bound to become a favorite in your breakfast repertoire.

Carrots, rich in beta-carotene, promote healthy vision and skin while adding natural sweetness and moisture to the waffles. Oats, loaded with fiber, keep you feeling fuller for longer and support digestive health. Eggs provide high-quality protein for muscle repair and growth, contributing to the waffles' structure and texture. Creamy coconut milk adds richness and flavor, alongside healthy fats for sustained energy. Baking powder helps the waffles rise to achieve that fluffy texture we all love, while a pinch of salt enhances the flavors and balances sweetness.

These Carrot Waffles are not only a delicious way to start your day but also a nutritious one. So, let's dive into the recipe and whip up a batch of these wholesome delights!

Prep time	Cook time	Total time	Serving
15 min	9 min	24 min	6 waffles

Ingredients

- 1 Cup oat flakes
- 1 Cup shredded carrots
- 1 Egg
- 1/4 Cup coconut milk
- 1 Tbsp baking powder
- Pinch of salt

Preparation

- In a mixing bowl, combine oat flakes, shredded carrots, egg, coconut milk, baking powder, and a pinch of salt.
- Mix the ingredients until well combined and the batter is smooth. Preheat your waffle iron according to manufacturer instructions.
- Once the waffle iron is hot, pour enough batter onto the iron to cover the waffle grid.
- Close the waffle iron and cook until the waffles are golden brown and crispy.
- Carefully remove the waffles from the iron and serve hot.
- Optionally, serve with toppings like maple syrup, yogurt, or fresh fruit.

Enjoy your delicious carrot waffles!

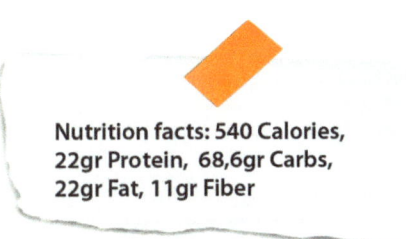

Nutrition facts: 540 Calories, 22gr Protein, 68,6gr Carbs, 22gr Fat, 11gr Fiber

Lentil Bagels

Letil Bagels

Lentils offer a range of health benefits, and incorporating them into your breakfast routine with protein-packed lentil crepes can be a smart choice. These crepes are not only delicious but also nutritious, with just four simple ingredients. With each serving containing only 126 calories per crepe, they provide a guilt-free indulgence. Lentils are rich in protein, making them a great addition to any meal, especially breakfast, as they can help keep you feeling full and satisfied throughout the morning. Additionally, lentils are packed with fiber, vitamins, and minerals, contributing to overall health and well-being. Try these lentil crepes as a healthy breakfast option and experience the benefits for yourself.

Note: You can store any leftover crepes in an airtight container in the refrigerator for up to three days. Simply reheat them in a lightly greased pan before serving.

Calorie-Conscious Tip:
To further reduce calories, you can skip the egg and use a flax egg (1 tablespoon ground flaxseed mixed with 3 tablespoons water) as a vegan alternative.

Nutrition facts: 540 Calories, 22gr Protein, 68,6gr Carbs, 22gr Fat, 11gr Fiber

Ingredients

- 2 Cups of raw lentils
- 1 Cup of Greek yogurt or vegan yogurt (optional)
- 4 Eggs
- Salt
- 1 Tablespoon of baking powder
- Coconut oil

Preparation

- The night before preparing the bagels, soak the lentils in water.
- Ensure you have a bagel tray ready.
  On the following day:
- Drain the lentils and set them aside.
- Preheat your oven to 350°F (175°C).
- Grease the bagel tray with coconut oil.
- Combine the following ingredients in your blender:
  - Eggs   - Yogurt   - Lentils   - Salt   - Baking powder
- Process the ingredients in your blender at medium speed for one minute.
- Spread the mixture evenly on your greased tray.
- Sprinkle poppy seeds or your preferred seeds on top of the mixture.
- Bake the bread in the oven for 45 to 60 minutes.
- The bread is ready when you insert a knife into it and it comes out clean.

These values are estimates and may vary depending on the specific brands of ingredients used and any variations in the recipe. For more precise nutrition information, you may want to use a nutritional calculator with the exact quantities of ingredients you plan to use.

Prep time	Cook time	Total time	Serving
5-10 min	45 min	55 min	6-8 bagels

Plantain Crepes

Looking for a breakfast that combines exotic flavors with comforting familiarity? Look no further than these delightful Plantain Crepes with Monster Cheese! In addition to satisfying your taste buds, these indulgent crepes offer a plethora of health benefits, making them a guilt-free indulgence to kick start your day.

These Plantain Crepes are packed with nutrient-rich ingredients. Plantains provide essential nutrients like potassium, magnesium, and vitamins A and C, supporting heart health, digestion, and immunity. Rolled oats offer fiber for digestive health and steady energy levels, while eggs provide high-quality protein and essential amino acids. The use of Himalayan salt adds trace minerals crucial for fluid balance and nerve function. Bananas contribute natural sweetness and energy-boosting carbohydrates, along with vitamins B6 and C. Meanwhile, Monster Cheese, despite its indulgent reputation, offers calcium for strong bones and protein for muscle health.

Incorporating plantains into your breakfast routine via these delicious crepes is not only a flavorful choice but also a nutritious one. Whether you're looking to indulge without guilt or seeking a satisfying breakfast that fuels your body, these Plantain Crepes with Monster Cheese offer the perfect balance of taste and nutrition. So, dive into these warm, cheesy crepes and start your day on a deliciously healthy note!

Nutrition facts: 146 Calories, 5,8gr Protein, 23gr Carbs, 2,6gr Fat, 383mg Sodium, 2,6gr Fiber

Ingredients

- 1 ripe plantain
- 1 ripe banana
- 1 cup rolled oats
- 2 eggs
- 1 cup water
- 1 tbsp Himalayan salt
- 1 tbsp baking powder
- Monster cheese for folding the crepes

Preparation

- Peel the plantain and banana, then slice them into chunks. Place them in a blender or food processor.
- Add rolled oats, eggs, water, Himalayan salt, and baking powder to the blender.
- Blend until you have a smooth batter consistency. If it's too thick, you can add a bit more water.
- Heat a non-stick skillet over medium heat. Once hot, pour a ladleful of batter onto the skillet and spread it out evenly to form a thin crepe.
- Cook for about 2-3 minutes until bubbles start to form on the surface, then flip and cook for another 1-2 minutes until lightly golden.
- Place a slice of Monster Cheese on one half of the crepe while it's still in the skillet.
- Carefully fold the other half of the crepe over the cheese, creating a half-moon shape. Let it cook for another minute or until the cheese starts to melt.
- Repeat with the remaining batter.
- Serve your warm, cheesy plantain crepes with a drizzle of honey or maple syrup for sweetness, or a sprinkle of powdered sugar for an extra touch of decadence!

Prep time	Cook time	Total time	Serving
10 min	15 min	35 min	6 people

Morning Power Juice

Empower your days with the below ideas

Kickstart your day with our invigorating Morning Power Juice, carefully crafted to fuel your morning routine with a burst of energy and essential nutrients. Here's why it's the perfect addition to your mornings:

1. Natural Energy Boost: With a combination of ripe bananas, juicy mango, sweet pineapple, tangy lemon, and crisp green apple, this juice provides a natural energy boost to kickstart your day without relying on caffeine or artificial stimulants.

2. Vital Nutrients: Packed with essential vitamins, minerals, and antioxidants from the fresh fruits and celery, this juice nourishes your body and supports overall health and wellness.

3. Hydration: The hydrating properties of the fruits in this juice help replenish your body's fluids after a night's sleep, ensuring you start your day feeling refreshed and revitalized.

4. Digestive Support: The fiber-rich ingredients like celery and apple promote healthy digestion, helping to keep your digestive system running smoothly and preventing sluggishness.

5. Immune Boost: The vitamin C from the lemon and other fruits in this juice provides a natural immune boost, helping to protect your body from illness and keeping you feeling your best.

6. Antioxidant Power: Loaded with antioxidants from the variety of fruits, this juice helps combat oxidative stress and inflammation, supporting overall health and longevity.

7. Delicious Tropical Flavors: Enjoy the delightful combination of tropical flavors that make this juice not only nutritious but also deliciously refreshing, making it a delightful way to start your day on a positive note.

Fuel your morning routine with our Morning Power Juice and experience the difference it can make in your energy levels, health, and overall well-being!

Pro tip: You can make a larger batch of this delicious juice and store it in the refrigerator for up to 24 hours. Shake well before serving if it separates. This juice is best enjoyed fresh, but if you're on the go, pour it into a travel-friendly bottle and take it with you for a revitalizing boost anytime, anywhere!

Ingredients

- 2 Ripe bananas
- 1 Juicy mango
- 1 Fresh celery stalk
- 1/2 Cup of sweet pineapple
- 1 Tangy lemon
- 1 Crisp green apple
- 2 Tbsp of ground cinnamon

Preparation

- Peel and slice the bananas and mango. Cut the celery stalk into smaller pieces.
- In a blender, combine the bananas, mango, celery, pineapple, lemon juice (squeeze out the juice), green apple (cored and sliced), and ground cinnamon.
- Blend all the ingredients until smooth and creamy.
- Pour the juice into glasses and serve chilled.
- Optionally, garnish with a slice of fresh lemon or a sprinkle of cinnamon for a touch of presentation.

Prep time	Blending time	Serving
10 min	2 min	3 people

Nutrition facts: 170-200 Calories, 2-3gr Protein, 23gr Carbs, 0,5-1gr Fat, 50-100mg Sodium, 6-8gr Fiber, 25-30gr Sugar

Enjoy the vibrant and refreshing flavors of this Morning Power Juice, and feel the energy radiate through your body!

Beets Juice

Beets Juice

Energize Your Morning with Power-Packed Juice!.
Rise and shine with a revitalizing elixir that will fuel your day with vigor and vitality! Our Power Morning Juice recipe is a delightful concoction crafted to infuse your mornings with an explosion of flavor and essential nutrients. This rejuvenating blend of beets, strawberries, cilantro, ginger, and lemon promises to awaken your senses and set the tone for a productive day ahead. Let's explore the wonders of this nourishing potion!

Benefits Summary:
1. Enhanced Energy: The dynamic combination of beets, strawberries, and lemon in this juice provides a natural energy boost, helping you kickstart your day with vitality and enthusiasm.

2. Nutrient-Rich: Packed with essential vitamins, minerals, and antioxidants from fresh ingredients like beets, strawberries, cilantro, ginger, and lemon, this juice nourishes your body from within, supporting overall health and well-being.

3. Immune Support: Ginger and lemon are renowned for their immune-boosting properties, while the antioxidants in strawberries and beets further strengthen your body's defenses, helping you stay resilient against illnesses.

4. Digestive Aid: Cilantro aids digestion and supports healthy gut function, while the combination of fiber-rich beets and hydrating lemon juice promotes digestive regularity and detoxification.

5. Anti-Inflammatory: The presence of ginger and cinnamon in this juice offers anti-inflammatory benefits, helping reduce inflammation and alleviate discomfort, promoting overall comfort and well-being.

6. Refreshing and Hydrating: With a base of water, this juice not only provides hydration but also refreshes and rejuvenates your body, leaving you feeling invigorated and ready to conquer the day.

7. Customizable and Delicious: Adjust the sweetness to your preference with honey and savor the delightful blend of flavors, from the earthy notes of beets to the tangy zest of lemon, making each sip a delightful experience tailored to your taste buds.

Indulge in the goodness of our Power Morning Juice to fuel your mornings with vitality, wellness, and the promise of a productive day ahead!

Tip: For a smoother texture, strain the juice through a fine mesh strainer. This step is optional but can be done if you prefer a silky consistency.

Start your day with a burst of energy and nourishment! This Power Morning Juice recipe is packed with vibrant flavors and wholesome ingredients to kickstart your morning. This invigorating blend of beets, strawberries, cilantro, ginger, and lemon will leave you feeling refreshed and ready to take on the day. Let's dive into the recipe and experience the goodness it has to offer!

Ingredients

- 2 Beets
- 7 Strawberries
- Small handful of cilantro
- 2 Lemons
- 1-Inch piece of raw ginger
- 1/4 Teaspoon of cinnamon
- 1 Tablespoon of honey (adjust to taste)
- 1 Cup of water

Preparation

- Wash the beets, strawberries, cilantro, lemons, and ginger under running water. This ensures that your ingredients are clean and free from any impurities.
- Peel and chop the beets and ginger. Removing the skin helps in achieving a smoother texture for the juice.
- Remove stems from strawberries and cut them in half. This makes it easier for the blender to break them down.
- Squeeze the lemons to extract their juice. Freshly squeezed lemon juice adds a zesty kick to the juice.
- Combine beets, strawberries, cilantro, ginger, lemon juice, cinnamon, honey, and water in a blender. The combination of flavors creates a delightful and balanced taste.
- Blend until smooth and well combined. The vibrant colors of the ingredients coming together indicate that your
- Power Morning Juice is almost ready!
- Adjust sweetness with honey, if desired. Taste the juice and add more honey if you prefer a slightly sweeter flavor.
- Pour into a glass and enjoy immediately. Freshly made juice ensures that you get the maximum nutrients and flavors.

Nutrition facts: 36 Calories, 0,5gr Protein, 9,25gr Carbs, 7gr Sugar, 1gr Fiber

Prep time	Blending time	Serving
10 min	2 min	3 people

Delicious Summer Snack

Delicious Watermelon Feta Rolls

The Watermelon-Feta Mint Rolls are a delectable summer snack that combines the sweetness of fresh watermelon with the savory tang of high-quality feta cheese, complemented by the refreshing aroma of mint leaves and finished with a drizzle of luscious balsamic glaze.

Inspired by a viral TikTok recipe, these elegant rolls are visually stunning and incredibly delicious, offering the perfect balance of sweet and savory flavors. To recreate this culinary masterpiece, you'll need fresh watermelon slices, rectangular blocks of feta cheese, fresh mint leaves, and a balsamic glaze.

Prep time	Blending time	Serving
10 min	2 min	3 people

Capture the beauty of your creation by snapping a photo and sharing it on Instagram with the hashtag #GourmetSummerBites. Get ready to receive a flurry of likes and comments from your friends and followers who will be amazed by your culinary skills.

Start your day with a burst of energy and nourishment! This Power Morning Juice recipe is packed with vibrant flavors and wholesome ingredients to kickstart your morning. This invigorating blend of beets, strawberries, cilantro, ginger, and lemon will leave you feeling refreshed and ready to take on the day. Let's dive into the recipe and experience the goodness it

Ingredients

- Fresh watermelon slices
- High-quality feta cheese, cut into rectangular blocks
- Fresh mint leaves
- Balsamic glaze

Preparation

- Begin by laying out the fresh watermelon slices on a clean surface. Choose ripe watermelon for the best flavor and texture.
- Place a rectangular block of high-quality feta cheese on each watermelon slice. The creamy feta will beautifully contrast with the juicy watermelon.
- Next, lay a few fresh mint leaves over the feta cheese. Mint adds a burst of freshness and complements the other flavors in the dish.
- Gently roll up each watermelon slice, securing the ingredients inside. The watermelon acts as a natural wrapper, creating a visually appealing and delightful package.
- Arrange the rolls on a serving platter, positioning them with care to showcase their vibrant colors and textures.
- To elevate the flavor profile, generously drizzle the rolls with a rich balsamic glaze. The balsamic glaze adds a sweet and tangy dimension that ties all the ingredients together.
- For an artistic touch, you can sprinkle some additional finely chopped mint leaves over the rolls. This will not only enhance the presentation but also provide an extra burst of minty aroma.
- Now, your Watermelon-Feta Mint Rolls with Balsamic Glaze are ready to be enjoyed! Serve them as an elegant appetizer at your next summer gathering or simply savor them as a light and refreshing snack.

Nutrition facts per serving (1 roll): 120-150 Calories, 5-6gr Protein, 25-30gr Carbs, 5-6gr Fat, 150-200mg Sodium, 2-3gr Fiber, 15-20gr Sugar

Creamy Shrimp Tacos

Creamy Shrimp Tacos

Ingredients

- 8 Corn tortilla soft tacos
- 1 Pound of fresh, succulent shrimp
- 2 Cups of shredded lettuce
- 2 Ripe, juicy tomatoes, diced
- 1 Creamy avocado, diced
- 1 Cup of shredded cheese
- 4 Ounces of smooth and tangy cream cheese
- 1 Small purple onion, diced

Preparation

Prepare the Shrimp:
- Rinse the shrimp under cold water and pat them dry with a paper towel.
- Season the shrimp with a blend of chili powder, cumin, garlic powder, and a pinch of salt.
- Heat a skillet over medium-high heat and cook the shrimp until they turn pink and tender, approximately 3-4 minutes per side.

Warm the Tortillas:
- Wrap the corn tortillas in a damp paper towel and microwave them for 30 seconds. Alternatively, warm them in a skillet over low heat for 30-60 seconds per side.

Add Creamy Base:
- Spread a dollop of cream cheese over each tortilla, creating a smooth and creamy foundation for your tacos.

Layer with Freshness:
- Place a generous handful of shredded lettuce on top of the cream cheese layer, adding a refreshing crunch to the tacos.

Pile on the Flavor:
- Spoon a flavorful medley of diced tomatoes, diced avocado, and purple onion over the lettuce, infusing the tacos with vibrant colors and tastes.

Complete with Shrimp and Cheese:
- Place a handful of the cooked shrimp onto each taco, ensuring every bite is filled with succulent goodness.
- Sprinkle shredded cheese over the shrimp, letting it melt slightly for an extra layer of deliciousness.

Serve and Enjoy:
- Your Creamy Shrimp Tacos are now ready to be savored.
- Serve them warm and watch as your family and friends delight in the explosion of flavors and textures with each mouthwatering bite.

Nutrition facts: 165 Calories, 11gr Protein, 8.8gr Carbs, 10.1gr Fat, 1.3gr Fiber

Peacock Fruit Salad

Peacock Fruit Salad

Nutrition facts per skewer in the fruit salad: 215 Calories, 54.5gr Carbs, 7.8gr Fiber, 39.5gr Sugar

Ingredients
- 1/2 pear, sliced
- 13 blueberries
- 13 golden apple cubes
- 13 tangerine slices
- 13 green grapes
- 13 red grapes
- 13 pineapple cubes
- 13 banana wheels
- 13 barbecue skewers

Preparation

Prepare the Fruits:
- Wash all the fruits thoroughly under cold water and pat them dry with a paper towel.
- Slice the pear into thin, semi-circular shapes. You can also cut out a small triangle from the pear skin to create a "beak" for the peacock. Assemble the Peacock's Body:
- Take a large serving plate or platter and arrange the pear slices in the shape of a peacock's body, with the narrow end pointing upwards and the wider end resembling the body.

Create the Tail Feathers:
- On the sides of the peacock's body, start inserting the barbecue sticks, leaving about 2-3 inches exposed on the bottom to act as the "feather's stem."
- Now, carefully skewer the fruits onto the exposed ends of the barbecue sticks to create the peacock's colorful tail feathers. Use the fruits in the following order: blueberry, golden apple cube, tangerine slice, green grape, red grape, pineapple cube, banana wheel. Repeat this pattern for each stick, and remember to keep the colors balanced and symmetrical on both sides.

Finishing Touches:
- Once all the tail feathers are in place, you can use an additional slice of pear or a round slice of tangerine to create the peacock's head. Place it at the narrow end of the body, making sure it slightly overlaps the pear slices.
- For the peacock's eye, you can use a small blueberry or a tiny piece of pineapple, gently pressing it into the head.

Serve:
- Place the finished peacock fruit salad on the table as a delightful centerpiece for your gathering or special occasion.

Palm Tree Fruit Salad

Palm Tree Fruit Salad

Ingredients

- 30 little kiwi slices
- 20 banana pieces
- 20 tangerine segments

Nutrition facts: 172 Calories, 103.8mg Vitamin C, 33.72mcg Vitamin K, 43.2gr Carbs, 337.6mg Potassium, 6.52gr Fiber

Preparation

- Base of the Palm Tree (Tangerine):
    - Take 20 tangerines and carefully peel them, removing any seeds or pith.
    - Gently separate each tangerine into segments and arrange them in the shape of a palm tree trunk on a large serving plate. This will serve as the base of the palm tree.
  Tree Trunk (Banana):
- - Peel the bananas and cut them into approximately 1-inch thick pieces.
    - Arrange the banana pieces vertically on top of the tangerine segments, forming the trunk of the palm tree. You can adjust the position of the bananas to make the trunk as straight as possible.
- Palm Tree Leaves (Kiwi):
    - Wash the kiwis thoroughly and slice them into thin rounds.
    - Starting from the top of the banana trunk, layer the kiwi slices in a fan-like manner to create the palm tree leaves. Continue until you have used all 30 kiwi slices, ensuring the leaves look lush and abundant.

Prep time	Cook time	Total time	Serving
15 min	9 min	24 min	5 people

Enjoy your creamy and comforting Green Pea Soup! It pairs wonderfully with a slice of crusty bread or a light salad.

Green Pea Soup

Green Pea Soup

Nutrition facts: 177 Calories, 6.7gr Protein, 11.4gr Carbs, 6.3gr Fat, 2.9gr Fiber

Ingredients

- 2 cups frozen green peas (or fresh if available)
- 1 medium-sized onion, chopped
- 2 garlic cloves, minced
- 1 medium-sized potato, peeled and diced
- 4 cups vegetable broth (or chicken broth if preferred)
- 1/2 cup heavy cream or coconut milk (for a vegan option)
- 2 tablespoons butter or olive oil
- Salt to taste
- Optional toppings: croutons, fresh herbs (such as parsley or mint), or a drizzle of olive oil

Preparation

- In a large pot or Dutch oven, melt the butter or heat the olive oil over medium heat.
- Add the chopped onion and minced garlic to the pot and sauté until the onions become translucent and fragrant.
- Add the diced potato to the pot and cook for a couple of minutes, stirring occasionally.
- Pour in the vegetable broth, bring it to a boil, and then reduce the heat to a simmer. Cook until the potatoes become tender, which should take about 10 minutes.
- Add the frozen or fresh green peas to the pot and cook for an additional 5 minutes. If using frozen peas, they should quickly thaw and cook through. If using fresh peas, they might take a bit longer to become tender.
- Once the peas are cooked, turn off the heat and let the soup cool slightly.
- Using an immersion blender or a regular blender, carefully blend the soup until it becomes smooth and creamy. If using a regular blender, blend the soup in batches, being cautious with the hot liquid.
- Return the blended soup to the pot (if using a regular blender), and stir in the heavy cream or coconut milk. Season with salt and pepper to taste, adjusting the seasoning as desired.
- Place the pot back on low heat and warm the soup through, but avoid boiling it.
- Serve the green pea soup hot in bowls, and if desired, garnish with croutons, fresh herbs, or a drizzle of olive oil.

Almond Banana Cake

Almond Banana Cake

Ingredients

- 3 ripe bananas, mashed
- 3 large eggs
- 1/4 cup honey or maple syrup
- 1/4 cup coconut oil, melted
- 1 teaspoon vanilla extract
- 2 cups almond flour
- 1 teaspoon baking powder
- 1/2 teaspoon baking soda
- 1/2 teaspoon cinnamon
- 1/4 teaspoon salt
- Optional: 1/2 cup chopped nuts (such as walnuts or pecans)

Preparation

- Preheat Oven: Preheat your oven to 350°F (175°C). Grease a 9-inch round cake pan or line it with parchment paper.
- Mix Wet Ingredients: In a large mixing bowl, combine mashed bananas, eggs, honey or maple syrup, melted coconut oil, and vanilla extract. Mix until well combined.
- Combine Dry Ingredients: In another bowl, whisk together almond flour, baking powder, baking soda, cinnamon, and salt.
- Combine Wet and Dry Ingredients: Gradually add the dry ingredients to the wet ingredients, stirring until just combined. Be careful not to overmix. If using chopped nuts, fold them into the batter.
- Bake: Pour the batter into the prepared cake pan and spread it evenly. Bake in the preheated oven for 30-35 minutes, or until a toothpick inserted into the center comes out clean.
- Cool: Allow the cake to cool in the pan for about 10 minutes, then transfer it to a wire rack to cool completely.
- Serve: Once cooled, slice and serve the banana cake. You can enjoy it as is or top it with a dollop of yogurt, whipped cream, or your favorite frosting.

Nutrition facts: 218 Calories, 5.8gr Protein, 10.8gr Carbs, 17.8gr Fat, 2.4gr Fiber

Oats and Banana Cookies

Oat and Banana Coockies

Ingredients
- 4 Ripe bananas
- 2 Cups of hearty oat flakes
- Decadent dark chocolate
- Crunchy chopped walnuts
- Sweet and shredded dried coconut

Oven Preheating: 350°F
Grease Your Cookie Pan with Coconut Oil

Preparation
- Begin by preheating your oven to 350°F for that perfect bake. Grease your cookie pan with a touch of coconut oil. It adds a delightful hint of tropical flavor!
- Peel and mash those ripe bananas into a sweet, creamy consistency.
- Carefully fold in the oats, using gentle, loving motions, until you have a dough-like mixture.
- Now, your mixture should resemble dough heaven!
- Shape the mixture into small, round balls and place them on your greased cookie pan.
- Flatten them slightly to create adorable cookie shapes.
- Pop those cuties into the oven and bake for a tantalizing 25 minutes. Your kitchen will soon be filled with mouthwatering aromas!
- While they're baking to perfection, melt some luxurious dark chocolate.
- As soon as your cookies are ready, drizzle them with the melted chocolate, sprinkle on the chopped walnuts for that satisfying crunch, and don't forget the shredded dried coconut to transport your taste buds to paradise!
- Allow them to cool for 30 minutes (if you can resist that long!), and get ready for a heavenly, guilt-free indulgence.
- Dive into these Oats and Banana Cookies and let your taste buds thank you later! A treat that's as easy to make as it is to enjoy.

Nutrition facts per cookies:
143 Calories, 3.6gr Protein,
21.4gr Carbs, 7.1gr Fat

Onion Soup

Onion Soup

Ingredients

- 4 large onions, thinly sliced
- 3 tablespoons butter
- 2 cloves garlic, minced
- 4 cups beef broth
- 1 cup chicken broth
- 1/2 cup dry white wine (optional)
- 1 tablespoon Worcestershire

Preparation

- Set your Instant Pot to the sauté function. Melt the butter in the pot and add the thinly sliced onions. Cook the onions, stirring frequently, until they are caramelized and golden brown, about 15-20 minutes.
- Add minced garlic to the pot and sauté for another 1-2 minutes until fragrant.
- Pour in the beef broth, chicken broth, and white wine (if using), scraping the bottom of the pot to release any browned bits. Add
- Worcestershire sauce, dried thyme, salt, and pepper to taste.
- Close the Instant Pot lid and set the valve to the sealing position.
- Cook on high pressure for 10 minutes.
- Once the cooking cycle is complete, allow the pressure to naturally release for about 10 minutes, then carefully switch the valve to the venting position to release any remaining pressure.
- Preheat your oven's broiler.
- Ladle the soup into oven-safe bowls. Top each bowl with a couple of baguette slices and a generous amount of shredded Gruyere cheese.
- Place the bowls on a baking sheet and place under the broiler for 2-3 minutes, or until the cheese is melted and bubbly and starting to brown.
- Carefully remove the bowls from the oven (they will be hot) and serve immediately.

Enjoy your delicious homemade Instant Pot French Onion Soup!

Nutrition facts: 335 Calories, 15.5gr Protein, 46gr Carbs, 33gr Fat, 8.1gr Fiber

Glossary

Millet Flour: A high-quality flour made from ground millet grains, known for its nutty flavor and gluten-free properties.

Oat Milk: A creamy, dairy-free alternative to cow's milk, made by soaking and blending oats with water.

Rolled Oats: Whole oat grains that have been steamed and flattened, commonly used in breakfast foods like oatmeal and pancakes for texture and nutrition.
Vanilla Extract: A flavoring made from vanilla beans soaked in alcohol, used to add a sweet, aromatic flavor to dishes.

Sea Salt: Salt derived from evaporated seawater, known for its distinct taste and mineral content.

Banana: A tropical fruit with a sweet flavor and creamy texture, often used as a natural sweetener and binder in recipes.
Egg: A staple ingredient in cooking and baking, providing structure, moisture, and richness to dishes.

Syrup: A sweet, viscous liquid made from concentrated sugar or natural sweeteners, commonly drizzled over pancakes for added sweetness.
Yogurt: A dairy product made by fermenting milk with bacterial cultures, often served as a topping or accompaniment to dishes for its creamy texture and tangy flavor.

Berries: Small, colorful fruits with a sweet or tart flavor, such as strawberries, blueberries, raspberries, or blackberries, commonly used as a topping for pancakes for freshness and added nutrients.

Almond Flour: A flour made from finely ground almonds, commonly used as a gluten-free alternative to wheat flour.

Sweetener: A substance used to add sweetness to food or beverages, such as granulated sugar, maple syrup, or honey.

Baking Powder: A leavening agent that helps baked goods rise by producing carbon dioxide gas when mixed with liquid and exposed to heat.

Salt: A crystalline substance composed primarily of sodium chloride, used to enhance flavor and season food.

Almond Milk: A dairy-free milk alternative made from almonds and water, often used by individuals with lactose intolerance or following a vegan diet.

Butter: A dairy product made from churning cream, commonly used in cooking and baking for its rich flavor and ability to add moisture and richness to dishes.

Oil: A fat derived from plants, seeds, or nuts, used in cooking for frying, sautéing, and baking.

Non-Stick Skillet: A frying pan with a surface coated with a non-stick material, such as Teflon, to prevent food from sticking during cooking.

Griddle: A flat cooking surface, often made of metal, used for cooking foods such as pancakes, eggs, and sandwiches.

Optional Toppings: Additional ingredients that can be added to the pancakes according to personal preference, such as fresh berries, sliced bananas, maple syrup, Greek yogurt, or chopped nuts.

Gluten-Free: Free from gluten, a protein found in wheat, barley, and rye, suitable for individuals with gluten intolerance or celiac disease.

Low-Carb: Low in carbohydrates, a dietary approach that restricts the intake of carbohydrates, often used for weight management or blood sugar control.

Nutritious: Containing essential nutrients, vitamins, and minerals that contribute to overall health and well-being.

Curry Rice: Cooked rice infused with curry spices, typically including turmeric, cumin, coriander, and other aromatic spices.

Crepe Batter: Mixture of cooked curry rice, eggs, water, and baking powder, blended to a smooth and creamy consistency for making crepes.

Non-stick Skillet/Crepé Pan: Cooking utensil used to cook the rice crepes, featuring a surface designed to prevent sticking without the need for excess oil or butter.

Spatula: Kitchen tool used for flipping and transferring the rice crepes during cooking.

Ladle: Utensil for pouring and measuring the batter onto the skillet, ensuring consistent portion sizes.

Shredded Chicken: Cooked chicken breast or thigh meat pulled into small, thin strips, often used as a topping for the rice crepes.

Vegetables: Assorted plant-based ingredients such as bell peppers, onions, spinach, or mushrooms, commonly used as toppings for the rice crepes.

Consistency: The thickness and texture of the crepe batter, adjustable by adding more water as needed to achieve the desired pouring and spreading properties.

Spices/Herbs: Flavoring agents added to the crepe batter to enhance the curry flavors, such as garlic powder, ginger, chili flakes, or cilantro.
Serving Suggestions: Ideas for how to enjoy the rice crepes, including topping recommendations and creative serving options.

Leftover Magic: Utilizing leftover curry rice to create a new and inventive dish, reducing food waste and adding variety to mealtime.

Bon Appétit: French phrase meaning "good appetite" or "enjoy your meal," used as a friendly wish for a delicious dining experience.

Quinoa: A highly nutritious grain known for its rich protein, fiber, and essential nutrient content. It is gluten-free and offers various health benefits, including improved heart health and digestive health.

Complete Protein Source: Indicates a food that contains all nine essential amino acids required by the body. Quinoa is a complete protein, making it valuable for vegetarians and vegans seeking alternative protein sources.

Heart-Healthy Fats: Fats that support cardiovascular health, found in foods like quinoa. These fats include omega-3 fatty acids and are beneficial for reducing cholesterol levels and inflammation, thus lowering the risk of heart disease.

Antioxidants: Compounds found in foods like quinoa that help protect cells from damage caused by free radicals. Antioxidants, such as flavonoids, contribute to overall health and well-being.

Fiber: A type of carbohydrate found in plant-based foods like quinoa that supports digestive health by promoting regular bowel movements and maintaining a healthy gut microbiome.

Satiety: The feeling of fullness and satisfaction experienced after eating. Quinoa's combination of protein and fiber helps increase satiety, making it beneficial for weight management.

Glycemic Index: A measure of how quickly a food raises blood sugar levels after consumption. Quinoa has a low glycemic index, meaning it does not cause rapid spikes or crashes in blood sugar levels.

Cooking Spray: A product used to coat cooking surfaces lightly to prevent food from sticking. It is often used as a low-calorie alternative to oil or butter.

Airtight Container: A container designed to prevent air from entering or escaping, commonly used for storing food to maintain freshness.

Reheat: The process of warming up cooked food before serving. Quinoa Crepes can be reheated gently in a skillet or microwave for a fresh taste.

Chickpeas: Nutritious legumes rich in protein, fiber, and essential vitamins and minerals.

Protein: A macronutrient essential for building and repairing tissues, including muscles.

Carbohydrates: Macronutrients providing energy to the body, found abundantly in chickpeas.

Iron: A mineral crucial for transporting oxygen in the blood and supporting overall health.

Magnesium: An essential mineral involved in various biochemical reactions in the body, including energy production and muscle function.

Folate: Also known as vitamin B9, folate is important for cell division and DNA synthesis.

Blood sugar: The concentration of glucose in the bloodstream, regulated by the slow-release carbohydrates in chickpeas.

Pourable batter: A mixture of ingredients with a consistency thin enough to pour easily.

Crepe pan: A specialized pan designed for cooking thin, delicate crepes.

Prep Time: The estimated time required to prepare the ingredients before cooking.

Cook Time: The estimated time required for cooking the crepes.

Total Time: The combined duration of preparation and cooking.

Nutrition Facts: Information about the nutritional content of the crepes per serving.
Calories: Units of energy derived from the crepes.

Fillings: Ingredients used to stuff or top the crepes, adding flavor and variety to the dish.

Nut butter: A spread made from ground nuts, offering a rich and savory filling option.

Scrambled eggs: A protein-rich filling option, perfect for adding a savory twist to the crepes.

Serving Size: The recommended portion of crepes per person.

Hearty breakfast: A satisfying and substantial morning meal.

Quick snack: A small, convenient bite to eat between meals.

Light lunch: A meal option that is not heavy or overly filling.

Oat Flour: Finely ground oats, used as a gluten-free alternative to wheat flour.

Dietary Fiber: A type of carbohydrate found in plant-based foods, essential for healthy digestion and maintaining bowel regularity.

B Vitamins: A group of vitamins that play essential roles in metabolism, energy production, and maintaining healthy skin, hair, and eyes.

Gluten Sensitivities: A condition where individuals experience adverse reactions to gluten, a protein found in wheat, barley, and rye.

Cholesterol Levels: The amount of cholesterol in the blood, which can impact heart health and increase the risk of cardiovascular diseases if elevated.

Cardiovascular Diseases: Disorders affecting the heart and blood vessels, such as heart disease, stroke, and hypertension.

Non-Stick Skillet/Griddle: Cookware with a surface designed to prevent food from sticking during cooking.

Total Fat: The total amount of fat in a food, including saturated, unsaturated, and trans fats.

Saturated Fat: A type of fat found in various foods, known to raise cholesterol levels and increase the risk of heart disease when consumed in excess.

Cholesterol: A waxy substance found in the blood, with high levels linked to an increased risk of heart disease.

Sodium: A mineral essential for fluid balance and nerve function, but excessive intake can contribute to high blood pressure and heart disease.

Spinach: Leafy green vegetable known for its vibrant color and nutritional value.
Free-range eggs: Eggs laid by hens that roam freely outdoors, often considered to have superior taste and nutritional quality.

All-purpose flour: Versatile flour suitable for various baking and cooking purposes.
Whole milk: Milk containing all its natural fat content, typically with a creamier texture and richer flavor.

Munster cheese: A type of soft cheese originating from France, known for its smooth texture and mild flavor.

Blender/food processor: Kitchen appliances used to blend or process ingredients into a smooth consistency.

Preparation: Steps involved in preparing the crepe batter and cooking the crepes.
Cooking: Process of heating and cooking the crepes on a skillet until they are golden brown.

Conclusion: Final remarks and encouragement for enjoying the finished dish.

Gastronomic adventure: Experience of exploring and enjoying the culinary world.
Symphony of flavors: Combination of diverse tastes that complement each other harmoniously.

Epicurean bliss: State of pure pleasure and enjoyment derived from fine food and drink.

Indulging: Treating oneself to something luxurious or enjoyable.

Appetizer: Small dish served before the main course as an introduction to a meal.

Luxurious brunch: Lavish mid-morning meal often featuring rich and indulgent foods.

White wine: Alcoholic beverage made from fermented grapes, often served chilled and paired with savory dishes.

Delicate textures: Subtle and refined mouthfeel of the crepes.

Culinary marvels: Extraordinary and impressive creations in the realm of cooking.

Green Peas Bread: A unique bread recipe that incorporates soaked green peas, vegan yogurt, eggs, salt, and baking powder to create a flavorful and nutritious loaf.

Soaked Green Peas: Green peas that have been soaked overnight to achieve tenderness before blending into the bread mixture.

Vegan Yogurt: A dairy-free alternative to traditional yogurt, adding creaminess to the bread mixture.

Eggs: Provide high-quality protein and essential amino acids, contributing to the texture and richness of the bread.

Pinch of Salt: Enhances flavor in the bread mixture.

Loaf Pan: The container used for baking the Green Peas Bread, ensuring even distribution of the mixture.

Preheat: To heat the oven to a specified temperature before placing the bread mixture inside for baking.

Blender: Kitchen appliance used to combine and blend the soaked green peas, vegan yogurt, eggs, salt, and baking powder into a smooth mixture.

Golden Crust: The desirable outer layer of the bread that forms during baking, adding a crunchy texture to each bite.

Slice: Portion of bread cut from the loaf, revealing the flavors and textures of the Green Peas Bread.

Tangy: Describes the slightly sour or acidic taste profile contributed by the vegan yogurt to the bread.

Richness: Refers to the luxurious texture and flavor imparted by the inclusion of eggs in the bread mixture.

Gourmet Adventure: An enriching and indulgent culinary experience, emphasized in the context of enjoying the Green Peas Bread.

Enchanting Flavors: Captivating and delightful taste sensations offered by the Green Peas Bread, inviting enjoyment and appreciation.

Happy Baking: A cheerful expression encouraging enjoyment and success in the baking process of the Green Peas Bread recipe.

Cassava: A versatile root vegetable commonly used in culinary applications. It is naturally gluten-free and rich in fiber, vitamins, and minerals.

Cassava Flour: Flour made from the cassava root. It is gluten-free and adds texture, flavor, and nutritional value to recipes.

Texture: The consistency or feel of a food product, influenced by ingredients such as cassava flour.

Dough: A mixture of flour, water (or other liquid), and other ingredients, such as egg, butter, and milk, used as a base for baked goods.

Nutty Flavor: A taste characteristic often associated with certain ingredients like cassava flour, adding depth and richness to dishes.

Binding: The process of holding ingredients together in a cohesive mixture, facilitated by the properties of cassava flour.

Cheese Balls: Small, round snacks or appetizers made from dough cheese, shaped into balls, and baked until golden brown.

Mozzarella Cheese: A semi-soft Italian cheese with a mild flavor and smooth texture, commonly used in cooking and baking.

Salted White Cheese: A type of cheese with a salty taste and white color, often used in Latin American cuisine.

Shredded Cheese: Cheese that has been grated or shredded into small pieces, used for coating or topping dishes like cheese balls.

Wax Paper: A type of paper coated with wax on both sides, used for lining baking trays to prevent sticking.

Cookie Oven Tray: A flat, rectangular tray used for baking cookies and other small baked goods in the oven.

Baking Temperature: The temperature at which food is baked in the oven, typically measured in Fahrenheit (°F) or Celsius (°C).

Baking Time: The duration for which food is baked in the oven until fully cooked or golden brown.

Instructions: Step-by-step directions for preparing a recipe, including preheating the oven, mixing ingredients, and baking.

Kneading: The process of working dough by pressing, folding, and stretching to develop gluten and create a uniform texture.

Manageable Consistency: The desired state of dough that is easy to handle and shape into balls.

Oven Tray Arrangement: The positioning of dough balls on the oven tray before baking.

Enjoy: A term used to express pleasure or satisfaction in consuming delicious treats like cheese balls made with cassava flour.

Lentils: Small, lens-shaped legumes that come in various colors and are a rich source of protein, fiber, vitamins, and minerals.

Protein-Packed: Refers to foods that are high in protein content, providing essential amino acids necessary for building and repairing tissues.

Crepes: Thin pancakes made from a batter consisting of flour, eggs, milk, and sometimes other ingredients, cooked in a skillet or crepe pan.

Indulgence: Refers to enjoying something pleasurable or luxurious, often in moderation.

Vitamins: Essential micronutrients required for various bodily functions, including growth, metabolism, and immunity.

Minerals: Inorganic compounds necessary for bodily functions such as bone health, nerve function, and fluid balance.

Guilt-Free: Refers to consuming something without feeling remorse or negative consequences, often used to describe healthy food choices.

Serving: A specific portion of food intended for one person.

Skillet: A flat-bottomed pan with sloping sides, typically used for frying, sautéing, or cooking pancakes and crepes.

Non-Stick: A surface that prevents food from sticking during cooking, often made with materials like Teflon.

Food Processor: A kitchen appliance with interchangeable blades and disks used for chopping, mixing, and blending food.

Grease: To coat a cooking surface with a thin layer of fat to prevent sticking.

Toppings: Additional ingredients added to a dish for flavor, texture, or decoration.

Refrigerator: An appliance used for preserving food at low temperatures to slow down spoilage.

Vegan: Refers to a diet and lifestyle that abstains from consuming animal products.

Flax Egg: A vegan alternative to eggs made by mixing ground

flaxseed with water, often used as a binding agent in baking.

Plant-Based: Refers to foods derived from plants, typically emphasizing whole, minimally processed ingredients.

Essential Nutrients: Nutrients that the body cannot produce on its own and must be obtained from food sources.

Batter: A mixture of ingredients used in cooking, typically consisting of flour, liquid, and other ingredients.

Cheesy Quinoa Crepes: A dish made by combining quinoa batter with assorted cheeses and fillings, cooked into thin crepes.

Pepper jack cheese: A type of cheese known for its spicy flavor, commonly used in Mexican cuisine.

Swiss cheese: A type of cheese known for its mild, nutty flavor and characteristic holes.

Preparation Steps: Sequential instructions for making the cheesy quinoa crepes, including soaking, blending, cooking, and filling.

Non-stick pan: A cooking utensil designed to prevent food from sticking during the cooking process.

Golden brown: A desirable color indicating the completion of cooking, often associated with a crispy texture.

Capturing: Taking a photograph of the finished dish.

Tag: A label used on social media platforms to categorize content.

Hashtag: A word or phrase preceded by a hash sign (#), used on social media platforms to identify messages on a specific topic.

Brunch: A late morning meal combining elements of breakfast and lunch.

Melty: The quality of becoming soft and gooey when heated, often used to describe cheese.

Goodness: A term used to express the delightful taste or quality of food.

Experiment: To try out different combinations or variations.

Culinary masterpiece: An exceptionally well-prepared dish.

Green peas: Small, spherical seeds harvested from the pod of a pea plant, often used in cooking for their sweet flavor and vibrant color.

Oat flakes: Rolled or crushed oats, commonly used in breakfast dishes, baking, and as a thickening agent in recipes.

Coconut milk: A creamy liquid extracted from the grated flesh of mature coconuts, used as a dairy alternative in cooking and baking.

Blend: To mix all ingredients together using a blender until a smooth consistency is achieved.

Pan: A flat, round cooking utensil with slightly raised edges, typically made of metal, used for frying, sautéing, and other cooking methods.

Coconut oil: A cooking oil extracted from the kernel or meat of mature coconuts, commonly used for frying and baking due to its high smoke point and unique flavor.

Dollop: A small, rounded portion or blob of a substance, often used to describe adding a spoonful of an ingredient onto a surface or into a mixture.

Ladleful: The amount of liquid or semi-liquid that a ladle can hold, typically used as a unit of measurement in recipes.

Swirl: To move or rotate a pan or utensil in a circular motion, spreading the batter or other substances evenly across a surface.

Shredded Mexican cheese: A blend of cheeses commonly used in Mexican cuisine, typically consisting of cheddar, Monterey Jack, and sometimes other varieties, shredded into small pieces for easy melting and topping.

Fold: To gently combine ingredients by repeatedly turning one part over another, typically done to incorporate delicate ingredients without deflating them.

Serve: To present food or a dish to be eaten, often accompanied by utensils or condiments.

Broccoli: A green vegetable related to cabbage, with dense clusters of tight green flower buds.

Himalayan Salt: A type of rock salt mined from the Punjab region of Pakistan, known for its pink color and distinct flavor.

Mixing Bowl: A bowl used for combining ingredients, typically in cooking or baking.
Maple Syrup: A sweet syrup made from the sap of maple trees, often used as a topping for pancakes, waffles, and other breakfast foods.

Delicious: Having a pleasing taste or flavor that is enjoyable to eat.

Natural Energy Boost: A surge in energy derived from the natural sugars and nutrients present in fruits like bananas, mangoes, pineapple, lemon, and green apple, providing vitality without the use of caffeine or artificial stimulants.

Vital Nutrients: Essential vitamins, minerals, and antioxidants vital for maintaining health and wellness, abundant in fresh fruits like bananas, mangoes, pineapple, lemon, green apple, and celery.

Hydration: The process of replenishing bodily fluids, facilitated by the water content in fruits such as mangoes, pineapple, lemon, green apple, and celery, aiding in feeling refreshed and revitalized.

Digestive Support: Assistance in maintaining healthy digestion, attributed to the fiber-rich content of ingredients like celery and apple, ensuring smooth functioning of the digestive system.

Immune Boost: Enhancement of the body's immune system,

primarily through the intake of vitamin C found in fruits such as lemon, aiding in defense against illnesses and promoting overall well-being.

Antioxidant Power: The ability to counteract oxidative stress and inflammation within the body, provided by the diverse array of antioxidants present in fruits, contributing to longevity and overall health.

Delicious Tropical Flavors: Pleasing taste sensations reminiscent of tropical climates, derived from the combination of fruits like mangoes, pineapple, lemon, and green apple, making the juice both nutritious and refreshingly delightful.

Ground Cinnamon: Finely powdered cinnamon obtained from the bark of Cinnamomum trees, adding a warm and slightly sweet flavor profile to the juice.

Pro tip: Expert advice or additional suggestion provided to enhance the preparation, preservation, or enjoyment of the recipe, such as storing the juice in the refrigerator for up to 24 hours or carrying it in a travel-friendly bottle for on-the-go consumption.

Garnish: Optional decoration or embellishment added to enhance the presentation or flavor of the dish, suggested in this recipe with a slice of fresh lemon or a sprinkle of cinnamon.

Travel-friendly bottle: A portable container suitable for carrying beverages while traveling, suggested for transporting the juice for consumption outside the home.
Revitalizing Boost: A rejuvenating surge of energy and refreshment provided by consuming the Morning Power Juice, contributing to a revitalized state of being.

Beets: Root vegetables with a deep red color, known for their earthy flavor and high nutritional content, including vitamins, minerals, and antioxidants.

Strawberries: Small, red berries with a sweet and slightly tart flavor, rich in vitamin C, fiber, and antioxidants.

Cilantro: A fragrant herb with citrusy notes, commonly used in culinary dishes for its fresh flavor and potential health benefits, including aiding digestion.

Ginger: A pungent and spicy root commonly used in cooking and traditional medicine for its anti-inflammatory properties and digestive benefits.

Lemon: Citrus fruit known for its tart flavor and high vitamin C content, used in cooking, beverages, and as a natural remedy for various health issues.

Cinnamon: A spice derived from the inner bark of trees, prized for its warm and sweet flavor, often used in cooking and beverages and known for its potential health benefits, including anti-inflammatory properties.

Honey: A natural sweetener produced by bees from the nectar of flowers, valued for its unique flavor and potential health benefits, including antibacterial properties and antioxidant content.

Water: A transparent, tasteless, and odorless liquid essential for life, used as a base in the juice recipe to adjust consistency and provide hydration.

Immune Boosting: Activities or substances that enhance the body's immune response, helping to defend against infections and illnesses.

Digestive Regularity: The consistent and efficient movement of food through the digestive tract, essential for nutrient absorption and waste elimination.

Detoxification: The process of removing toxins and harmful substances from the body, often associated with improving overall health and well-being.

Anti-Inflammatory: Actions or substances that reduce inflammation in the body, potentially alleviating pain and promoting better health outcomes.

Nutrients: Substances found in food that are essential for growth, development, and maintaining health, including vitamins, minerals, and macronutrients like carbohydrates, proteins, and fats.

Vibrant: Full of life, energy, and color; used to describe the appearance and characteristics of fresh fruits, vegetables, and other foods.

Watermelon: A juicy and sweet fruit with a high water content, often enjoyed in the summer months for its refreshing taste.

Feta Cheese: A brined cheese made from sheep's milk or a combination of sheep and goat's milk, known for its tangy flavor and crumbly texture.

Mint Leaves: Fragrant green leaves from the mint plant, commonly used to add freshness and a subtle minty flavor to dishes and beverages.

Balsamic Glaze: A thick, syrupy reduction of balsamic vinegar, often sweetened with sugar or honey, used to add a sweet and tangy flavor to dishes.

Rectangular Blocks: Square or rectangular-shaped portions of feta cheese, typically cut for convenience and presentation in recipes.

Serving Platter: A large plate or dish used for presenting and serving food, often chosen for its aesthetic appeal.

Drizzle: To pour or sprinkle a thin stream of liquid over food, typically for flavor enhancement or decorative purposes.

Ripe: Fully matured and ready to eat, often used to describe fruits and vegetables at their peak of flavor and ripeness.

Presentation: The arrangement and visual display of food on a plate or platter, emphasizing aesthetics and appeal.

Corn Tortilla Soft Tacos: Thin, flatbread made from ground maize (corn), typically used to wrap various fillings, popular in Mexican cuisine.

Shrimp: Small, edible crustaceans with a delicate flavor and tender texture, commonly used in seafood dishes.

Lettuce: Leafy green vegetable with a mild flavor and crisp texture, often used in salads and as a taco topping for its freshness.

Tomatoes: Juicy, red fruits with a tangy-sweet flavor, commonly used in various cuisines for their versatility and nutritional value.

Avocado: Creamy, green fruit with a buttery texture and mild flavor, often used in Mexican cuisine for its richness and health benefits.

Cream Cheese: Soft, spreadable cheese with a mild flavor and creamy texture, often used in both sweet and savory dishes for its richness.

Purple Onion: Variety of onion with purple skin and white flesh, known for its mild flavor and crisp texture when raw, commonly used in salads and as a garnish.

Chili Powder: Spice blend made from dried chili peppers, often mixed with other spices like cumin and garlic powder, used to add heat and flavor to dishes.

Cumin: Aromatic spice with a warm, earthy flavor, commonly used in various cuisines, including Mexican, to add depth and richness to dishes.

Garlic Powder: Ground, dried garlic cloves, used as a seasoning to add a savory flavor to dishes without the hassle of peeling and chopping fresh garlic.

Microwave: Kitchen appliance that uses electromagnetic radiation to or heat food quickly and efficiently.

Medley: A varied mixture or assortment, often used to describe a combination of different ingredients or flavors.

Savor: To enjoy or appreciate the taste and flavor of food or drink slowly and appreciatively.

Mouthwatering: Describes food that looks or smells so delicious that it stimulates the production of saliva in the mouth, indicating a strong desire to eat it.

Pear: A sweet and juicy fruit with a characteristic bell shape and a green or yellow skin.

Blueberries: Small, round berries with a dark blue-purple color and a sweet-tart flavor.

Golden apple cubes: Cubes of apple with a golden-yellow color, sweet taste, and crisp texture.

Tangerine slices: Thin slices of a small citrus fruit similar to mandarin oranges, known for their sweet and tangy flavor.

Green grapes: Small, round fruits with a green skin and a sweet, slightly tart flavor.

Red grapes: Small, round fruits with a red or purple skin and a sweet, slightly tart flavor.

Pineapple cubes: Small cubes of pineapple, a tropical fruit with a sweet and tangy taste and a fibrous texture.

Banana wheels: Slices of banana with a round shape and a creamy texture, known for their sweet flavor.

Barbecue skewers: Long, thin sticks used for skewering and grilling food, typically made of wood or metal.

Note: This glossary provides definitions for ingredients used in the Peacock Fruit Salad recipe to aid in understanding the preparation process.

Onion: A bulb vegetable with layers of edible leaves, commonly used as a flavoring agent in various cuisines due to its pungent taste and aroma.

Garlic: A pungent bulb composed of several small cloves, widely used in cooking for its distinct flavor and aroma.

Potato: A starchy tuber vegetable often used in cooking, prized for its versatility and ability to add texture and substance to dishes.

Vegetable Broth: A flavorful liquid made by simmering vegetables, herbs, and spices in water, used as a base for soups, stews, and sauces.

Chicken Broth: A savory liquid made by simmering chicken bones, vegetables, and aromatics in water, commonly used as a base for soups and sauces.

Heavy Cream: A rich dairy product with a high fat content, commonly used in cooking and baking to add richness and creaminess to dishes.

Olive Oil: A type of oil extracted from olives, widely used in cooking for its flavor and health benefits.

Pepper: A spice made from dried and ground peppercorns, commonly used in cooking to add heat and flavor to dishes.

Croutons: Small pieces of toasted or fried bread, often seasoned and used as a garnish for soups and salads.

Herbs: Plants used for flavoring, garnishing, or medicinal purposes, often added to dishes either fresh or dried.

Parsley: A leafy herb with a fresh, mild flavor, commonly used as a garnish or flavoring agent in various dishes.

Mint: A fragrant herb with a refreshing taste, commonly used in cooking and beverages for its cooling effect and distinctive flavor.

Immersion Blender: A handheld kitchen appliance used to blend ingredients directly in the cooking vessel, making it convenient for soups and sauces.

Regular Blender: A kitchen appliance with a container and blades used for blending and pureeing ingredients into smooth mixtures.

Creamy: A texture characterized by a smooth, thick consistency, often achieved by adding dairy or thickening agents to a dish.

Crusty Bread: Bread with a firm, crisp crust and a soft interior, often enjoyed as an accompaniment to soups and salads.

Yuca Flour (Cassava Flour): A gluten-free flour made from the root vegetable yuca (also known as cassava). It adds a unique flavor and texture to baked goods.

Oat Flakes (Rolled Oats): Whole oat grains that have been steamed and then rolled into flat flakes. They provide a nutty flavor and hearty texture to recipes.

Cold Water: Water chilled to a low temperature, used to bind the ingredients together and form the dough.

Egg Wash: A mixture of beaten egg and sometimes water or milk, brushed onto pastries before baking to give them a shiny, golden-brown crust.

Pastry Cutter: A kitchen tool with curved blades used to cut fat (such as butter) into dry ingredients when making pastry dough.

Parchment Paper: A non-stick paper used to line baking sheets or pans, preventing food from sticking and making cleanup easier.

Rectangle: A four-sided shape with opposite sides equal and four right angles.
Triangle: A three-sided polygon with three angles.

Roll and Fold: A technique used in pastry-making to create layers of dough by rolling it out, folding it into thirds, and repeating the —

Croissant: A crescent-shaped pastry made of layered yeast-leavened dough, typically buttery and flaky.

Baking Sheet: A flat, rectangular metal pan used for baking foods in an oven.
Cool: Allowing baked goods to reach room temperature before serving to prevent burns and improve flavor.

Spreads: Accompaniments for baked goods, such as butter, jam, or honey, used to enhance flavor.

Greek Yogurt: A thick, creamy yogurt with a tangy flavor, commonly used in cooking and baking for its rich texture and probiotic benefits.

Flaxseed Flour: Ground flaxseeds used as a gluten-free alternative to traditional flour, providing a nutty flavor and added nutrients like omega-3 fatty acids and fiber.

Curry: A blend of spices commonly used in South Asian cuisine, typically including turmeric, cumin, coriander, and other spices, to add flavor and aroma to dishes.

Chia Seeds: Nutrient-rich seeds derived from the Salvia hispanica plant, often added to dishes for their high fiber, protein, and omega-3 fatty acid content, as well as their ability to thicken and gel liquids.

Wire Rack: A metal rack with evenly spaced wires used for cooling baked goods by allowing air to circulate around them, preventing condensation and ensuring even cooling.

Insertion Test: A method of checking the doneness of baked goods by inserting a knife or toothpick into the center and ensuring it comes out clean, indicating that the item is fully cooked.

Cooling: Allowing baked goods to come to room temperature after removing them from the oven, which helps them set and develop their final texture.

Instagram Hashtag: A word or phrase preceded by the "#" symbol used on the social media platform Instagram to categorize posts and make them discoverable to users interested in a specific topic or theme.

Power Green Morning Juice: A revitalizing beverage aimed at providing a burst of energy in the morning, made from a combination of nutrient-rich greens and fruits.
Celery: A fresh vegetable used in the recipe, offering a crisp texture and subtle flavor, rich in vitamins and minerals.

Mango: A juicy tropical fruit included in the recipe, adding sweetness and vitamins to the beverage.

Immune Function: The body's ability to defend against pathogens and maintain health, supported by the nutrients in the juice.

Digestion: The process of breaking down food and absorbing nutrients, aided by the fiber and nutrients in the ingredients.

Healthy Skin: Supported by the vitamins and antioxidants present in the juice, contributing to a glowing complexion and overall skin health.

Wellness: A state of overall health and well-being, promoted by the nutrients and benefits of the Power Green Morning Juice.

Energy Boost: Provided by the natural sugars and nutrients in the juice, offering a revitalizing start to the day.

Sources

https://www.webmd.com/

https://www.healthline.com/

https://medlineplus.gov/

https://www. nedininglovers.com